MetaThink™

for exemplary performance

The Exemplary Worker Book Series

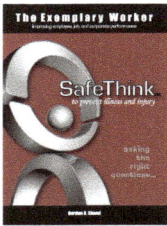

SafeThink™ ...to prevent illness and injury

SafeThink is a structured critical thinking strategy you can use to identify, predict, and control hazardous situations before, during, and after completing work. This cognitive-based safety strategy can be used on the fly, at work, at home, at play, and while driving. *SafeThink* also provides strategies for you to remain focused on your tasks.

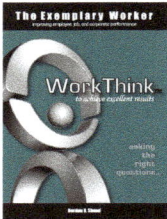

WorkThink™ ...to achieve excellent results

WorkThink is a thinking strategy you can use to achieve quality results with the least amount of effort. It usually takes little extra effort to do quality work instead of inferior work. *WorkThink* also emphasizes understanding the expectations of your supervisor, team leader, and customers so that you can achieve the excellent results they expect.

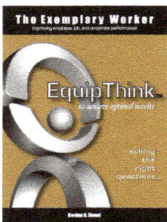

EquipThink™ ...to achieve optimal results

EquipThink is a thinking strategy for you to use tools, mobile equipment, and stationary equipment effectively and efficiently. The goals are for you to achieve the desired results with minimal stress on equipment, to conserve energy, and to extend equipment life. The input–process–output thinking strategy, in conjunction with identifying critical variables, is used to achieve optimal results.

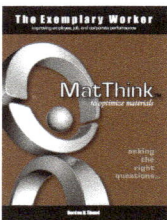

MatThink™ ...to optimize materials

MatThink is a thinking strategy you can use to make the most effective use of materials. The thinking strategy applies to recovering, processing, modifying, applying, transporting, and storing materials. Because equipment and materials are usually closely related, the input–process–output thinking strategy, in conjunction with identifying critical variables, is used to optimize material recovery and use.

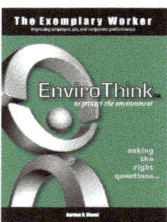

EnviroThink™ ...to protect the environment

Both industry and individuals have a responsibility to protect the environment. *EnviroThink* is a critical thinking strategy you can use to identify and respond to environmental issues for any job position that you might hold. *EnviroThink* helps you think through your work by asking yourself specific questions relating to environmental issues important to organizations.

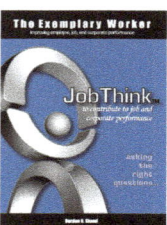

JobThink™ ...to contribute to job and corporate performance

Exemplary workers understand what is important to their organizations. They know the issues critical to business success and where to focus their efforts. *JobThink* addresses the critical thinking strategies you can use to identify what is important for job and corporate performance.

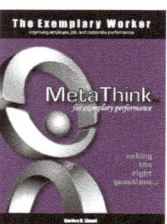

MetaThink™ ...for exemplary performance

MetaThink applies some of the thinking strategies addressed in previous books in different ways and also addresses new thinking strategies useful for the workplace. You can use these thinking strategies, along with the detailed thinking strategies addressed in other books of this series, to achieve exemplary performance.

The Exemplary Worker Book Series

"Rarely can workers from any sector access self-paced instructional materials that are easy-to-use, step-by-step guides to workplace learning. *The Exemplary Worker* book set is an exception. These books offer a good breadth of learning for workers in contexts ranging from: exemplary performance; job and corporate performance; results optimization; and work excellence. With meticulous organization, these essential training references are helpful guides for workers seeking to improve their performance. With prefaces designed to help trainers/instructors assist workplace learners, these books use critical thinking strategies that identify what matters to workers and supervisors considering people, equipment, materials, environments, and organization in concert."

—**Eugene G. Kowch, Ph.D.**, Leading Complex and Adaptive Learning Systems/Organizations, University of Calgary, Canada

"The power of thinking in determining our safety, health, and welfare is obvious, but how to manage such cognition or self-talk for injury prevention, self-motivation, and self-improvement is not so obvious. Answers are provided in this action-focused series of self-help books on *The Exemplary Worker* by Gordon D. Shand. He offers much practical information for leadership, safety, and well-being. Each of these books provides critical and structured thinking strategies for optimizing performance on several fronts, from improving safety and productivity in the workplace to actively caring as a teacher, parent, or friend."

—**E. Scott Geller, Ph.D.**, author of The Psychology of Safety Handbook; Alumni Distinguished Professor, Virginia Tech; Senior Partner, Safety Performance Solutions

"These are very practical books. I, myself, have been interested in the fundamental processes of human thinking. For creativity there is Lateral Thinking. For exploration there is the parallel thinking of the Six Thinking Hats. For perception there is the CoRT school programme. *The Exemplary Worker* series of books provide frameworks for focused thinking about specific situations. The frameworks guide the thinker to deal with the situation instead of messing about. That is why the books are so practical."

—**Dr. Edward de Bono**, Author of Lateral Thinking and Six Thinking Hats and creator of CoRT

The Exemplary Worker Book Series

MetaThink™

for exemplary performance

Gordon D. Shand

HDC Human Development Consultants Ltd.
PO Box 4710, Edmonton, AB, Canada T6E 5G5
www.hdc.ca
www.safethink.ca

MetaThink™

Library and Archives Canada Cataloguing in Publication
Shand, Gordon D.
    MetaThink for exemplary performance / Gordon D. Shand.
(The exemplary worker book series)
ISBN 978-1-55338-057-3
    1. Excellence. 2. Employees. 3. Organizational effectiveness.
4. Critical thinking. I. HDC Human Development Consultants
II. Title. III. Series: Exemplary worker
HD5650.S52 2014   658.3'152   C2014-902767-7

Published by HDC Human Development Consultants Ltd.

Published in Canada

HDC *Human Development Consultants Ltd.*

Website: www.hdc.ca
E-mail: hdc@hdc.ca
Phone: (780) 463-3909

Acknowledgements

Developing *The Exemplary Worker* book series has been challenging and rewarding. I am certainly grateful for all the help I have received to produce quality products. Over one hundred people have contributed to the quality of the content and presentation.

Generally, I developed the first draft of the books working on evenings and weekends. I would blitz the first draft for a book—I produced the draft in a month to three months. During those times, my family's gracious support allowed me to concentrate on the task and to dialogue with them about the concepts. Once a first draft was produced, consultants in my firm carried out several edits as time allowed. HDC's Production Department developed illustrations and formats to produce a book ready for validation by industry. Because the people from industry volunteered their time and some validations were conducted in sequence, the validation process for each book took up to six months or more.

Many staff contributed to the development process. I would like to acknowledge those consultants who struggled to gather relevant content when working with customers—they gave cause to identify the thinking strategies used by exemplary workers and to develop the training for HDC consultants. Many thanks to the consultants who worked so diligently with me to produce the books. They were adamant in adhering to our standards for quality, even when I was burned out and wanted to put closure to a topic. Thanks to Janelle Beblow, Art Deane, Alice Graham, Jean MacGregor, and Bruno Schoenfelder for the wonderful edits and feedback. Thanks to Phil Jenkins, Kris Vasey, and Denise Hodgins for developing the illustrations, formatting the documents, and creating the book covers. Thanks to Maria Peck for coordinating the validations and field tests and proofing text. Their personal support, commitment to quality, and attention to detail are greatly appreciated.

I have been exceptionally fortunate to work with so many wonderful people from industry. They have been great mentors—they have made many contributions to my personal growth. A special thanks to nearly a hundred people who have volunteered their time to validate and field test the strategies.

Who is *The Exemplary Worker* series for?

The Exemplary Worker series benefits:

- **Individuals** who want to have outstanding performance

- **Apprentices and students** who want to work safely and effectively

- **Supervisors** who want staff to be more effective

- **Trainers** who want to contribute to improved corporate, job, and employee performance
- **Trades and technology instructors** who want their apprentices and students to work safely and effectively

- **Instructional designers** who want to ensure that training is relevant, useful, and practical

- **HR managers** who want to improve the development and retention of exemplary workers

- **Operations staff** who want to optimize production and minimize losses

Contents

MetaThink™

Table of Contents (continued)

Preface

In addition to being skilled, exemplary workers use a broad range of *critical thinking strategies* to maintain outstanding performance. Exemplary workers know what is important to their jobs and organizations—they put their efforts in the right places by doing the most important things, doing them effectively, and doing them efficiently. Because they know what is important to the job and the organization, they effectively coordinate their actions with others and make decisions in the best interest of their organizations. Knowledge and thinking skills empower workers to achieve exemplary performance, be flexible as workplaces continue to evolve, and provide leadership within the workplace.

Exemplary performance can have many benefits for you, the line worker, lead operator, foreman, or supervisor, including:
• increased job satisfaction
• being recognized by your peers and supervisors as an effective employee
• increased potential for keeping your job during slow economic times
• increased potential for receiving salary/wage increases or bonuses
• increased opportunity for new or different work assignments
• increased potential for promotion

Each of the seven books in *The Exemplary Worker* series focuses on one of five domains (**PEMEO**):
• **P**eople
• **E**quipment
• **M**aterials
• **E**nvironment
• **O**rganization

Loss and/or optimization (LO) are the main themes for the domains, creating the word **LO-PEMEO™**. LO-PEMEO stands for Loss and Optimization of People, Equipment, Materials, Environment, and Organization. As an example: **L**oss to **P**eople is illness and injury; **O**ptimizing **P**eoples' performance is working effectively and efficiently; **L**oss to **E**quipment is damage and shortened operating life; and **O**ptimizing **E**quipment is using equipment effectively and efficiently. The books place a strong emphasis on using **thinking strategies** and **asking quality questions**—the goals are to minimize losses and optimize performance of PEMEO.

The series of books addresses both loss and optimization of each domain. We recommend that you complete each of the first six books in the sequence. However, the books can be studied in any order without difficulty. The last book in the sequence, *MetaThink*, should be read last. *MetaThink* applies some of the thinking strategies addressed in previous books but in different ways and also addresses new thinking strategies useful for the workplace.

Introduction to *The Exemplary Worker* Series

Over the last twenty-five years, the process of discovering *what's important* for exemplary worker performance has gone full circle. The process began for me when I interviewed exemplary workers to identify relevant training content. My premise was that exemplary workers know what is important for people to do their jobs effectively. Over time, it became apparent to me that one of the reasons exemplary workers perform so well is that they use a set of generic thinking strategies. After starting a consulting firm to design and develop training, I developed a comprehensive internal training program for our consultants and technical writers who develop training programs. The training focused on using generic thinking strategies and critical questions to identify training content that helps workers perform effectively. With a lot of support, I have revised our consultant training program and made it available to the public for people to learn and refine their personal thinking strategies to be exemplary workers.

The Exemplary Worker books are presented as a series. The same concepts underlie all seven books. For example, a safety incident may cause harm to a person and result in other losses—work may be suspended, equipment and materials damaged, the environment harmed. The organization could also experience unpredicted costs and have its reputation harmed. This introduction provides a framework and the key concepts that apply to the series. The discovery process and happenstances that led to the development of *The Exemplary Worker* series are explained to provide a setting and context to give meaning to the underlying concepts.

The Discovery Process

For me, the real discovery process began in 1985 when I founded the consulting firm HDC Human Development Consultants Ltd. (HDC) to design and develop customized technical training programs. I believed that it was possible to develop quality training for any industry without having an in-depth understanding of the organization, its technology, or the tasks that its people perform. The premise was that a well-thought-out instructional design and development process combined with effective consulting skills would be sufficient.

As founder of the company, I felt that I was successful in providing leadership to identify training content important to my customers—customers often asked me to do additional work. If I could do the work well, then certainly others in the firm could as well and, for some deliverables, do better.

The Plan

The plan was that I would work with customers to develop the outline of the training program (curriculum) and identify critical content for the program. The training program would be documented in one of three ways:
- a list of specific courses
- a list of general training objectives
- a competency-based training profile

Competency-Based Training Profile

The following illustration is a *partial* example of a competency-based training profile. The profile is a visual presentation of the competencies (tasks and support knowledge) that specific work groups require to do their work safely and effectively.

MetaThink™					
ORIENTATION	Complete Company Orientation	Describe Roles and Responsibilities	Identify Local Structures and Facilities	Describe and Use Communication Systems	Identify Customers and their Expectations
SAFETY	Describe and Use Personal Safety Equipment	Review Safety Handbook	Complete First Aid Training	Decribe and Operate Personal Gas Monitors	
ENVIRONMENT	Describe Environmental Responsibilities	Describe and Store Hazardous Wastes	Describe and Monitor Gas Emissions	Take Waste Water Samples	Describe and Participate in Spill Response Exercises
GENERAL KNOWLEDGE AND SKILLS	Describe Flammable Gas Measurements	Use Portable Multi-Gas Monitor	Describe Reciprocating Compressors	Prepare Maintenance Requests	
ROUTINE TASKS	Carry out Routine Equipment Checks	Change Process Filters	Describe and Change Corrosion Coupons	Monitor and Adjust Inhibitor Injection	Perform Housekeeping
SITE-SPECIFIC KNOWLEDGE AND TASKS	Describe Remore Process	Start and Adjust Remore Process	Describe and Change Remore Output Parameters	Perform Emergency Shutdown of Remore Process	Shut down Remore Process for Maintenance

Critical content for each competency is a list of the key issues a buddy or supervisor would emphasize when coaching the trainee. The end product is a *scope document* listing the key issues and ensuring continuity between competencies—no overlaps or gaps in content. As an example of a scope document, here is a partial list of key issues for the competency *Purge Piping and Station Systems:*

- replacing one medium with another to prevent combustible or toxic condition
- important to prevent:
  - people being exposed to toxic gases
  - possibility of a fire
- piping should only be purged after system has been opened and exposed to a foreign substance
- stations purged in preparation for startup
- some stations have automatic purging for specific piping and equipment
- automatic purging sequence must be checked
- always purge in direction gas migrates (up or down)
- criteria for length of time to purge include volume, pressure, and amount of connected equipment

In a profiling workshop, I used a brainstorming technique with four to sixteen of the customer's employees to identify competencies and critical content. The workshops were mentally demanding. On the one hand, I was concerned that the scope of training and performance requirements be limited and only address competencies and content that were considered important to the workers, their supervisors, and the organization. On the other hand, I was concerned that critical issues affecting people and the business were not overlooked. During these workshop sessions, I was constantly searching for relevant, useful, and practical content. What do the workers do? Is there a special way of doing the task? How do they know they are doing a good job? What can go wrong? How can the equipment be damaged or its life shortened? What do you mean by product quality? What about safety and the environment? Does the organization have special policies and ways of doing business? What is important and to whom or what? What questions should I be asking the group? I did not have a clear set of criteria or a structured thinking process that I could use to provide leadership in identifying training content that was important to the worker and the supervisor.

Working with Subject Matter Experts (SMEs)

I certainly believed that asking quality questions was more important than providing content. Answers to the questions could be provided by the customer's experienced employees. The term *subject matter experts* (*SMEs*) is often used to refer to the organization's staff who provide content to training consultants and technical writers. Unfortunately, some SMEs, having in-depth knowledge of the tasks, technology, and the organization, had difficulties identifying content important for training. These SMEs expected consultants to provide leadership to identify relevant content. I soon discovered that my consultants often had difficulties in providing leadership to SMEs trying to identify content that was relevant, practical, and useful. When reviewing the first draft of training modules, information that would help trainees do their jobs more effectively, efficiently, and safely would often be missing. Nor would the supervisor's concerns always be addressed. Sometimes, information would be included that was of little value in helping workers do their jobs well and making decisions in the best interest of their organizations. When consultants asked me for direction as to the types of content that were relevant for training, I could not provide a comprehensive explanation. If the company was going to be successful in the future, I needed to find ways to define content that was relevant, practical, and useful—content that contributed to employee, job, and corporate performance.

Customer feedback gave me reason to believe that I was providing adequate leadership to identify relevant content; that I was asking quality questions. The truth of the matter was I did not have a formal list of types of question I should ask. In many ways, I was relying on intuition to ask the right questions. I needed to find a way to articulate a content gathering strategy that consultants could use with a variety of customers in different lines of business, different technologies, different hiring practices and performance expectations, and different ways of conducting business. I needed to find a way to identify the specific types of question consultants could ask SMEs to identify important training content—content that would help workers perform their jobs safely and effectively and contribute to meeting corporate objectives.

To help our training consultants and technical writers gain a better understanding of our customers, their businesses, goals, and concerns, I took consultants along to the competency-based profiling sessions. Listening to the group discussions and individual insights about the work and the business always provided learning beyond the information recorded in the program outline and scope document. This learning should be valuable when working with SMEs to identify detailed content for the training resources. Having this preliminary knowledge about the customer seemed to help some consultants be better at identifying relevant training content, but other consultants continued to struggle. I concluded that knowledge about the customer was valuable but didn't give consultants the strategies they needed to provide leadership when working with SMEs.

The Importance of Training Content Being Relevant to the Organization, Job, and Employees

Project reviews with customers were very useful for gaining ideas on how to improve services and products. Feedback from SMEs was that HDC consultants asked more questions than anyone they had ever worked with before. On the other hand, our consultants felt that they didn't ask enough questions because relevant information had been missed. The real issue was to ask fewer questions but more *quality* questions— questions that addressed issues that were important to employees, the job, and the organization. Certainly, customers strongly indicated that identifying relevant, useful, and practical content was the most important quality concern they had regarding the development of training resources. Customers also were adamant that consultants provide direction and leadership when working with SMEs to identify relevant content.

At the close of each project, I would ask the customer what additional training might be useful for consultants to help them be more effective at identifying relevant content. Suggestions included that consultants could increase their technical knowledge, or have a better understanding about safety management systems, environment management systems, or management styles. In response to suggestions, we began providing additional internal training using off-the-shelf technical training materials when possible. The additional training helped consultants to better understand what SMEs were telling them but only resulted in marginal improvements in consultants being able to provide leadership to identify relevant content. I concluded that the knowledge is useful but not sufficient in helping consultants (and workers) to identify issues important to employee, job, and corporate performance.

To compound the problem of identifying relevant content, expectations in industry were changing from developing entry level training (do as I tell and show you and don't ask why) to exemplary level training (maximizing productivity and making quality decisions) and every level between those two extremes. These changing expectations created difficulties in determining the content and amount of detail to include in training and keeping within training development budgets. Customers were upset if training materials included content they did not want and were not willing to pay for. Customers could also be disappointed if the training did not include content that they considered important. In many ways, the concerns consultants had in understanding the customer's expectations are the same concerns an employee new to a job would have.

When I had worked with exemplary workers, I discovered that one of their strategies was to confirm expectations. So we used the same strategy and built more confirmation checks into the development process to ensure the content was what customers wanted. Unfortunately, the confirmation checks were good at confirming that the documented content was what customers wanted but did not effectively address concerns about omissions of content important to customers (e.g., safety, equipment life).

Identifying Thinking Strategies Used by Exemplary Workers

Developing internal training for consultants to effectively identify relevant, useful, and practical content proved to be very difficult. Having consultants participate in the profiling sessions to learn about the customer, developing scope documents, providing technical and organization training, and building in confirmation checks had some value but weren't sufficient in helping them to provide leadership to identify relevant training content.

The instructional systems design models I was familiar with generally placed a strong emphasis on instructional development processes and only provided marginal direction and strategies on how to provide leadership to identify content that was important to customers. Certainly, the design of instruction and the nature of the content had an effect on each other. I suspected that there were instructional designs in which generic module structures and generic types of content would work for some types of technology and associated training outcomes. It would be several more years, after we had a large inventory of customized self-instructional modules, before we were able to develop a set of generic boilerplates (list of section and sub-section titles) for specific technologies and training outcomes. These *boilerplates* provided general structures for self-instruction and listed the types of content that *could* be included (but not necessarily included) in each section. No doubt, the SMEs that I worked with had mentally created their own boilerplates to be effective when working with specific types of equipment.

My initial effort to develop training to identify relevant content proved to be fairly impractical. Fortunately, several events provided me with the fundamental concepts needed to develop strategies that consultants could use to identify relevant content.

One of HDC's customers had a very demanding supervisor who was exceptionally analytical. In fact, he was by far the most powerful analytical thinker I have met. He was also driven to prevent anything negative from happening. He would always be analyzing situations and wanted to know all the *hows* and *whys* about every aspect of the instructional design that came to mind. Once a week I would make a personal visit to address his concerns. On one of those visits, he demanded to know what type of content should be addressed in the training. He said he asked our consultant the same question and the consultant's response was that *he would write self-instruction on anything as long as we told him the content*. Obviously, the consultant was not providing leadership when working with the SME to identify training content that would help the operators perform their work safely and effectively. For me, it was confirmation that our internal training was not very effective in helping our consultants to provide leadership.

My immediate response to his demand was to give some general criteria for identifying relevant content. *Well, safety, environment, equipment life, product quality, and customer satisfaction are important. Adhering to legislation and making decisions are important, too.*

There was a long silence—a lot of mental processing was going on in his head. Finally, he nodded and said, *Good. Let's tell the consultant and the senior operator what you just said.* The bottom line for this customer was that the training we were developing would contribute to his staff doing their work effectively and safely and making good decisions.

The interaction I had with that customer was the moment of discovery for me! The three-hour drive back to the office gave me time to reflect on what had just happened. Obviously, until I was asked, I had not been able to see the forest for the trees. Ask any business person what is important to their business success and he or she would give a list of areas of concern similar to the one I gave to my customer. No doubt the business person's list would be more extensive and include additional concerns affecting productivity and controlling losses—all businesses want to get the most out of their assets, including their people. Businesses prefer to have exemplary workers, workers that contribute to business success. Certainly, the training we develop for customers must help workers be effective in doing their jobs.

Creating the LO-PEMEO Model to Identify Relevant Training

I reflected on the thinking process I was using to identify relevant content when developing training profiles and scope documents. The questions that I had been asking myself during the sessions addressed the optimization and prevention of losses primarily to People, Equipment, Materials, Environment, and the Organization as a whole. Surely, the questions would take on meaning when the work environment was considered. And one way of assessing the work environment was to consider the conditions, actions, and events within the workplace that affect PEMEO.

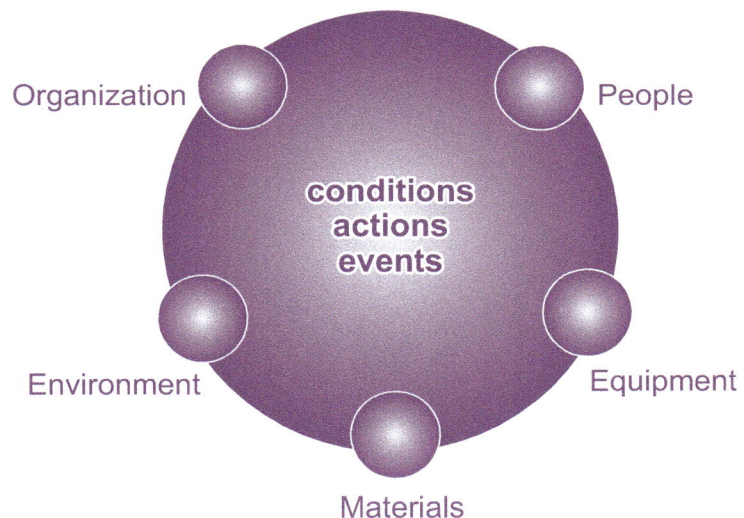

Most exciting for me, I could combine the concepts of optimization and controlling losses of organizational assets such as people and equipment to create a model and strategy for identifying relevant content. The LO-PEMEO model was born. Each of the five domains (people, equipment, materials, etc.) shown in the above illustration had potential for optimization and loss. An example of loss to people is illness and injury. Loss of materials when processing ore is the inefficient recovery of the desired products. Optimization of materials in construction is to use the right materials and maximize the use of the materials. The following illustration shows the combinations of loss and optimization of PEMEO.

LOSS					OPTIMIZATION	
Loss:	People	LP	P	OP	Optimization:	People
Loss:	Equipment	LE	E	OE	Optimization:	Equipment
Loss:	Materials	LM	M	OM	Optimization:	Materials
Loss:	Environment	LE	E	OE	Optimization:	Environment
Loss:	Organization	LO	O	OO	Optimization:	Organization

Exemplary workers consider the potential for Loss and Optimization of each domain of PEMEO (i.e., LO-PEMEO) while they work. So LO-PEMEO was used as the framework and structure for *The Exemplary Worker* series of books. For example, loss to people (LP) is safety—the book *SafeThink* focuses on using a structured critical thinking strategy to identify and predict hazardous situations to prevent illness and injury.

Interestingly, several years later, I was introduced to a loss control model created by Frank E. Bird that used PEME as an acronym. I have always wondered if it would have saved me a lot of effort if I had known of Bird's loss control model earlier. Or would that knowledge have put in place constraints such that I would never have created the LO-PEMEO model?

While driving back to my office, I thought about how fortunate I had been over the years to work with a lot of exemplary performers, many of them my SMEs. Our customers gave us SMEs who are exemplary workers because the belief is that exemplary workers know what is important for business success and will provide training content that is relevant to corporate, job, and employee performance. When I had asked the SMEs if there were any concerns about issues such as safety, equipment, or materials, they would often look at the ceiling and ponder for a while. If they said yes, they would go on and give me further clarification. If they said no, I would continue to ask different questions. When I thought about it, the questions that I asked SMEs usually focused on concerns about LO-PEMEO. I always wondered what the SMEs were thinking when they were looking at the ceiling and pondering the answers to my questions. Eventually, I asked them. Interestingly, different SMEs from different companies and lines of business had similar concerns. For example, damage to equipment often involved shock from a sudden change in physical forces or temperature. The sources for causing damage could be people, material, or any of the other three domains. In fact, *each domain has the potential to affect the other domains.* Whether the SMEs were aware of it or not, they were mentally searching for specific workplace concerns relating to LO-PEMEO. In many ways, even at the detailed level, *the thinking strategies of exemplary workers were similar and generic.* Certainly, being aware of one's own thinking strategies contributes to planning and working effectively and helps to communicate effectively when collaborating with others and mentoring apprentices.

Linking Corporate, Job, and Employee Performance

When organizations develop standards, procedures, and training, they want to realize an improvement in corporate performance. Improving *corporate performance* is often achieved by either filling a gap in performance or by preparing the organization to move towards new goals. The following illustration lists some criteria that can be used to measure corporate performance.

PERFORMANCE REPORT

Customer Satisfaction	UP
Production	UP
Product Quality	UP
Equipment Run Time	UP
Equipment Damage	DOWN
Energy Consumption	DOWN
Material Waste	DOWN
Personal Injuries	DOWN
Maintenance Costs	DOWN
Environment Damage	DOWN
Rework Time	DOWN

At the operational or job level, the supervisor also has concerns about performance. Within his or her roles, responsibilities, and authority, the supervisor is expected to maximize productivity and minimize losses. Improved *job performance* contributes to improved corporate performance. The supervisor therefore represents the concerns and goals of the organization and must use specific resources and assets (including people) to effectively achieve the goals. The supervisor must also be able to motivate, coordinate, and assign staff to effectively carry out the work. Furthermore, worker performance affects job performance which, in turn, affects corporate performance.

Employee performance affects business results. Employees are expected to work effectively and efficiently and make good use of materials and technology. Expectations of performance are articulated to line employees both orally and in writing. In turn, employees have concerns about understanding the expectations and working safely, effectively, and efficiently to meet the expectations. The following illustration is of a person new to a job asking questions relating to corporate, job, and employee performance issues.

What's important to the business?

What does the team leader expect of me?

What am I supposed to do?

How am I supposed to do it?

How do I know I've done well?

How does my work affect others?

Is there a better way?

What tools and equipment are used?

Could I get hurt?

Could I injure others?

Could I damage the equipment?

Does this product affect the environment?

How much waste is acceptable?

How can I prevent...?

Will the customer be satisfied?

What should I do if ...?

What would happen if ...?

Do I have the authority to take action?

What action?

Whom should I inform?

What does ...?

How does ...?

What caused ...?

What is the reason?

What are the consequences for ...?

What questions should I be asking?

What answers do I need?

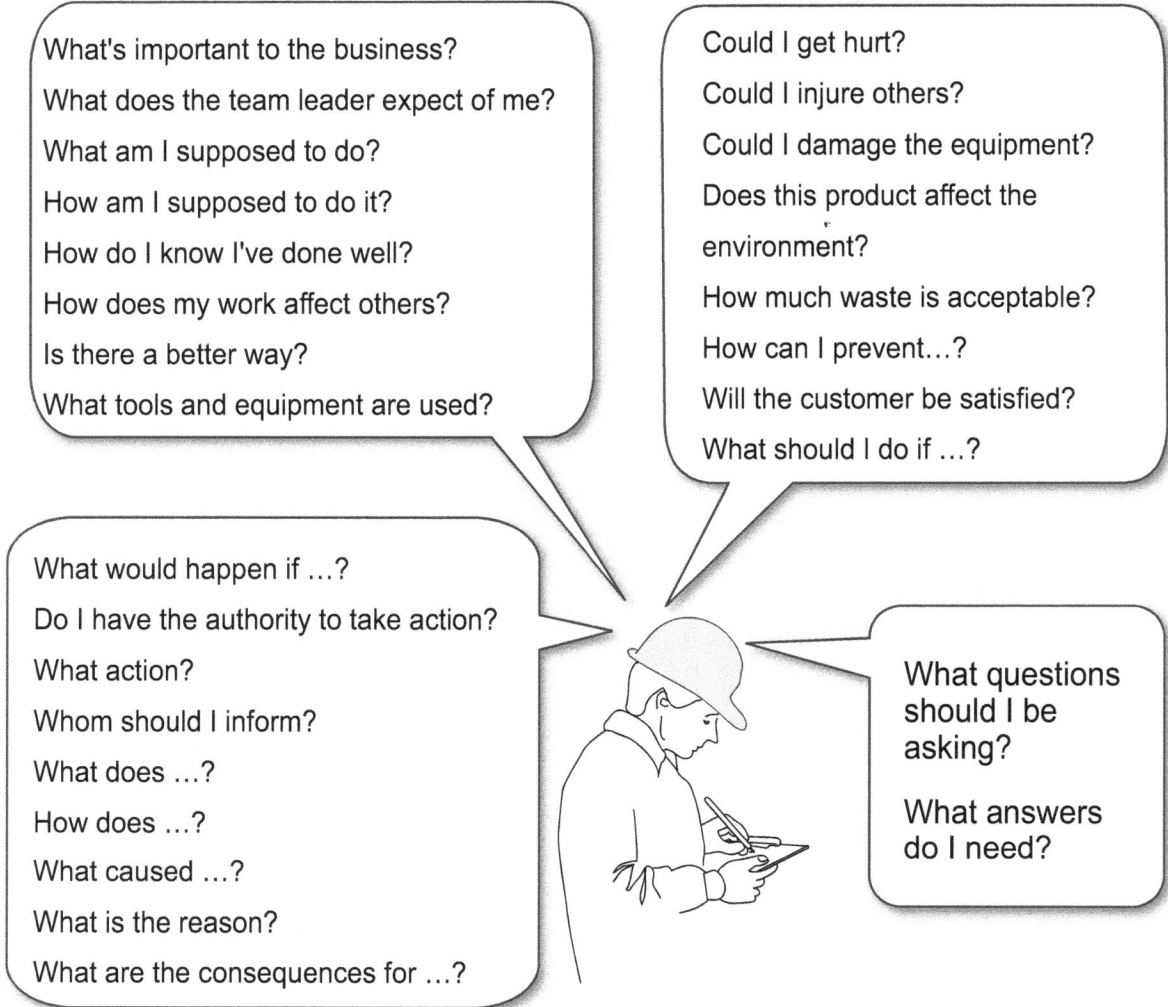

Many of the questions are generated by the LO-PEMEO strategy and focus on performance:

- What is important?
- What are the issues?
- What questions should I ask?

The person new to the job needs answers to the questions in the illustration to quickly learn to do that job effectively and efficiently. Interestingly, two employees with similar experiences and skills who are new to a job can perform quite differently. One employee will be uncertain about the work and become stressed if work conditions change. The other employee will initiate actions and make good work-related decisions for the organization within a few weeks. One of the factors that makes the difference in performance between the two employees is the knowledge about what is important to job and corporate performance. Understanding *what is important* provides criteria for focusing one's efforts and for making decisions. LO-PEMEO is a good start in identifying what is important to the organization. Although many of the issues identified by LO-PEMEO are generic, each organization has its own business strategies, resources, and priorities. As such, each organization could place a different emphasis on each issue identified by LO-PEMEO. And that's why asking the *right* questions is so valuable. Questions focus on key issues; the answers to the questions are unique to the organization, workplace, and specific circumstances. *The Exemplary Worker* series provides many of the questions that workers need to ask of themselves and of others to achieve exemplary performance.

Understanding Organizations for Exemplary Worker Performance

Exemplary workers understand what is important to the organization so that they put their efforts in the right places, do the right things, and make good decisions in the best interests of their organizations. For workers to have exemplary performance, they need to have an understanding of organizations in general, and a specific understanding of their own organization. Training and performance consultants also need to have a general understanding of organizations to be effective at developing customized training—training that is relevant, useful, practical, and reflects the organization for what it is. There is a lot of literature on organizations but most of it is more complex than training consultants need. Generally, the literature does not directly address issues important to designing and developing customized training for industry.

So, what issues are important? For consultants at HDC (and exemplary workers in other organizations) to be effective, they must be able to identify and understand organizational issues from different points of view. Imagine a roomful of statues facing in different directions. The room has many doors, each opened by a different work group or discipline. Each doorway has a different view of the statues.

For consultants to get a broader understanding of the organization, they need to view the statues from different doors. Ideally, consultants would walk around the statues to get many different points of view. The consultant must be prepared to consider different points of view within a specific organization to be effective at understanding the organization and identifying issues important to employee, job, and corporate performance.

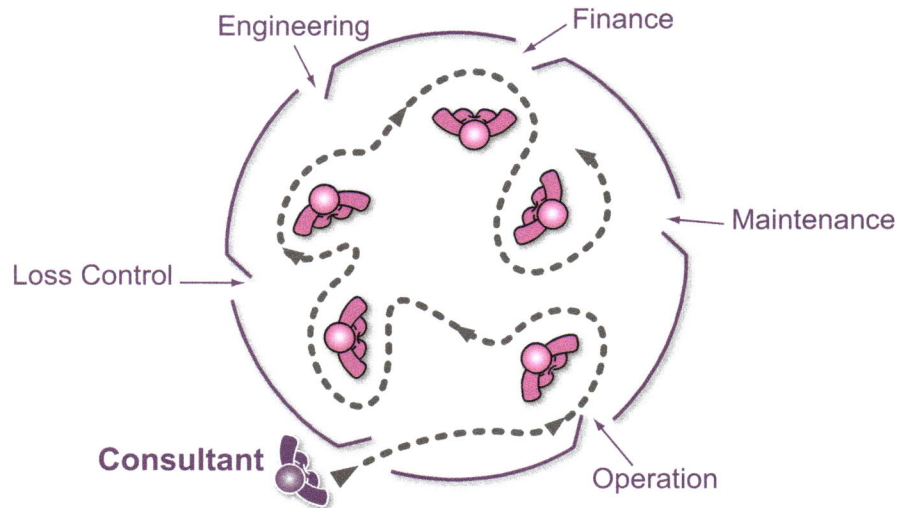

Both exemplary workers and training/performance consultants benefit from an understanding of relationships between business resources, organizational structure, business strategies, corporate objectives, and performance standards. Exemplary workers gain an understanding as to how their line of work fits into the organization as a whole. In doing so, they appreciate how their work affects others and they potentially make better use of organizational resources. This understanding about organizations also helps training consultants and technical writers to be more effective at designing and developing training that is customized, reflects the business, and has excellent value for the customer.

The approach I take with consultants to learn about organizations is to pretend to build a new business. Would the line of business be a service or a product? What is the mission? If the business is a service, then performing tasks is the main way to generate revenue and tools/equipment provide support for carrying out the work. If the line of business is to use technology to make products, then the technology dictates many of the tasks that workers must do. Having resources to achieve specific results is essential but not sufficient for business success. The resources must also be managed effectively. The following illustration identifies some key constituents of a business.

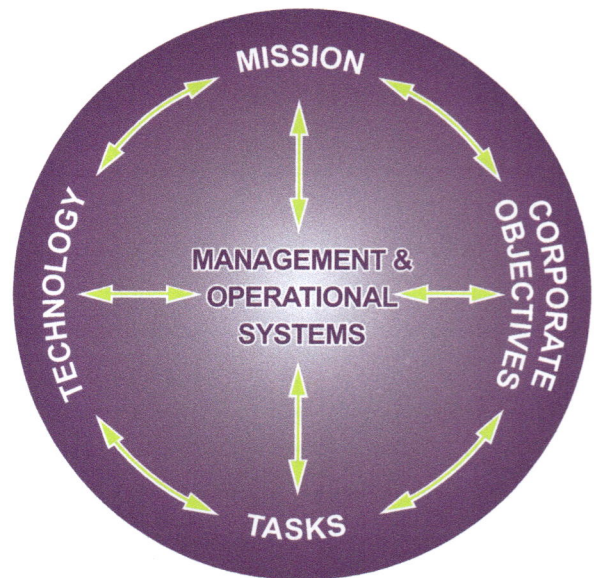

The book *JobThink* uses the previous model to provide a practical way for workers to understand organizations. This understanding helps workers to effectively focus their efforts and make decisions in the best interests of their organizations.

Of particular interest are the *corporate objectives*. Corporate objectives provide direction for using technology, performing tasks, and coordinating work to effectively achieve the corporate mission. The following table lists areas of concern, common to many organizations, for which corporate objectives may be developed.

Areas addressed by Corporate Objectives

• safety	• quality	• public image
• environment	• waste control	• public disruption
• legislation	• loss control	• reputation
• equipment reliability and life	• cost control	• communication
• equipment optimization	• customer satisfaction	• teamwork
• energy use		

For a specific organization, a list of corporate objectives can be generated by expanding the organization's strategic business objectives or by using LO-PEMEO. Some companies issue strategic business objectives to provide direction to employees as to where to put their energy and focus for business success. Strategic business objectives identify what the organization must do well to be successful. For example, leaders in an organization may believe that it is essential for business success to have reliable service and satisfied customers. Organizations may identify five to eight strategic objectives. Within a department, the list of objectives (or goals) may be expanded in more detail to address issues specific to the department's mandate.

The expanded list of corporate objectives can also be generated using LO-PEMEO—each of the items in the above table relates to one or more of the LO-PEMEO domains.

Corporate objectives are fundamental to exemplary performance because they define what is *important* to the organization, the job, and workers. Corporate objectives provide a ***formal link*** between organizational goals and worker performance. Workers can use corporate objectives as criteria for working effectively and efficiently and for making decisions in the best interest of their organizations. Training consultants and technical writers can use corporate objectives to identify relevant, useful, and practical training content. Refer to my book, *Interviewing to Gather Relevant Content for Training* for:

• information about applying critical thinking skills to identify relevant content for training

• an interviewing process that consultants and technical writers can use to interview SMEs to gather relevant content

MetaThink™

Developing Training to Identify What is Important to Employee, Job, and Corporate Performance

With the LO-PEMEO and business models, I could now develop training for consultants to provide leadership to identify relevant content. The LO-PEMEO model was the most practical approach to use to structure the training because it relates directly to work and job issues. The organizational model can be integrated into the training on loss and optimization of organization, LO-O. For the training on these models to be useful, the training needs to be flexible and apply to a broad range of work, technology, and organizations. The training must also provide strategies for people to think through their work. That is what exemplary workers do—they think through their work. And, the thinking processes are generic so they apply to all types of industries, work environments, and jobs.

All of the training to identify relevant content is founded on using thinking strategies. An emphasis is placed on *concepts* and *generalities* to maintain a broad application of the thinking strategies. Furthermore, the thinking involves asking questions relating to LO-PEMEO. Asking questions is important to maintaining the broad application of the thinking strategies and helping people remain mentally engaged. Asking the *right* questions is often more important than finding the answers, because if the right questions are asked, answers can usually be found— answers that contribute to exemplary employee, job, and corporate performance.

Over several years, I developed training for all the combinations of LO-PEMEO. I also expanded the training to include consulting processes and a performance and training model to design, develop, and implement competency-based training and performance management systems. I was very fortunate to have excellent support from staff to edit and refine the training. HDC staff made important contributions to the training content and presentation. And, after the training resources were in use, we refined them further.

Developing *The Exemplary Worker* Series

After the HDC consultants' training resources had been used for ten years, I decided to go full circle and modify the resources for general use. A major rewrite was required; the new audience was very broad and the lines of work very diverse. The instructional design content had to be deleted. New and different examples of applying the thinking strategies were required for the books. To help the reader, each book required new learning activities. Exemplary workers in industry needed to field test and validate the content. Staff also needed to make major contributions to ensure the quality of each book. It took over six thousand hours to develop *The Exemplary Worker* series. In addition, industry has volunteered more than a thousand hours to field test and validate the content.

The Exemplary Worker series has many suggestions to help you not only be aware of your own thinking strategies but also help you to refine your strategies to achieve exemplary performance. You will also be better at mentoring others to perform better.

Gordon D. Shand
Edmonton, Alberta
Canada

Training Objectives

Upon completion of this book, you will be able to apply various thinking strategies to identify what is important to corporate, job, and employee performance and to determine the best course of action. You will be able to:

- Apply a business process
- Apply corporate goals to determine what is important
- Assess issues from different job perspectives
- Use variables to identify what is important
- Use reasons, causes, and consequences to determine the best course of action
- Apply LO-PEMEO to effectively contribute to optimizing organizational performance and minimizing losses
- Ask the right questions

Introduction

This book is one of *The Exemplary Worker* series of books. Books in the series all focus on using critical thinking strategies to identify **what is important** to employees, the job, and the organization. Each book focuses on one of five domains (**PEMEO**):

P People

E Equipment

M Materials

E Environment

O Organization

Within each book, loss and/or optimization (LO) are the main themes, hence the word LO-PEMEO™:

Themes	Books
L-P Loss to People (Safety)	*SafeThink* Use a structured thinking strategy to identify and predict hazardous situations.
O-P Optimize People's Performance	*WorkThink* Work effectively and efficiently.
LO-E Loss and Optimization of Equipment	*EquipThink* Use tools and equipment effectively and efficiently.
LO-M Loss and Optimization of Materials	*MatThink* Use materials effectively and efficiently.
LO-E Loss and Optimization of the Environment	*EnviroThink* Protect the environment.
LO-O Loss and Optimization of the Organization	*JobThink* Contribute to job and corporate performance.
LO-PEMEO Use thinking strategies for the workplace	*MetaThink* Integrate thinking strategies for exemplary performance.

The fundamental premise of LO-PEMEO is to develop thinking strategies for *asking questions* that focus on issues affecting business success. By asking yourself questions, you remain alert. By seeking answers, you continually learn and become more effective in the workplace and adaptable to changes. The big question is: *What questions should I ask?* The questions identified in LO-PEMEO help you to ask many of the *right* questions to do your job effectively and efficiently with minimal effort.

For this book, the term *meta* means encompassing and more developed. Ideally, you should complete the first six books before reading this one. Some key concepts from the first six books are reinforced in this book to help you integrate the thinking strategies. New thinking strategies are also addressed. When you use a broad set of thinking strategies, you are more effective in assessing issues, determining what is important, and focusing your efforts. The goal is for you to work effectively and in ways that contribute to job and organizational performance.

The learning activities that are integrated into this book provide you with opportunities to apply these critical thinking strategies to your job, workplace, and personal activities. Each learning activity relates to specific concepts addressed in this book. It is recommended that you complete each learning activity as you progress through the book. The Job Aid lists the key questions you need to ask and for which you need to seek answers to be an exemplary worker.

Certainly, a powerful thinking strategy that exemplary workers use is to apply LO-PEMEO throughout the work day. And one of the thinking strategies addressed in this book is to use all parts of LO-PEMEO simultaneously so that you are rigorous at identifying *what is important* to your work, the job, and the organization.

While LO-PEMEO is a powerful strategy, there are times when exemplary workers find it useful to use additional thinking strategies. In this book, you will practice applying the following thinking strategies:

Apply a business process: This thinking strategy has three major steps: *discover, decide, deliver.* The process is useful for any department and job and can be used with both internal and external customers. The beauty of the process is that there is agreement between stakeholders as to the best course of action so that expectations are clearly understood and met.

Use corporate objectives/goals: Corporate objectives or goals are a wonderful way of determining what is important to the job and the organization. The book *JobThink* emphasizes the value of using corporate objectives or goals to make decisions in the best interest of your job and organization. This book revisits the use of corporate goals because corporate goals apply to other thinking strategies addressed in this book.

Assess issues from different job perspectives: People from different departments and jobs have different mandates. Each person could have a different understanding of what is important to the job and the organization. Differences in mandate and not understanding how a specific mandate affects others can cause conflict between people from different departments and jobs. This book reinforces the concept of *business context* addressed in the book *JobThink*. The business context provides the foundation for determining different points of view that others in the organization may have. An emphasis is placed on understanding the concerns of your supervisor or boss so you can better focus your efforts in meeting his or her expectations.

Use variables: The book *EquipThink* emphasizes the value of identifying equipment variables that affect your job and the decisions you make. This basic concept of using variables is expanded to include all the PEMEO domains so you can perform your work more effectively.

Use reasons, causes, and consequences to determine why variables are important: For variables to have meaning, you must know why the variables are important to the corporation, the job, and your work. The answers to the question: *Why are these variables important?* can be identified by examining the reasons, causes, and consequences of a specific condition, action, or event in the workplace. By continually determining reasons, causes, and consequences before, during, and after completing work, you can perform your work more effectively. You can also be more effective at making *good* decisions that contribute to business success and minimize losses.

Apply LO-PEMEO: The LO-PEMEO strategy is a powerful tool for identifying what is important to corporate, job, and employee performance. The strategy focuses on work conditions, actions, and events to identify consequences for PEMEO and ways to improve efficiencies and reduce the risk of losses. If you have completed all the books, you have learned each part of the LO-PEMEO strategy one at a time. Applying all parts of the strategy at once is a rigorous way of determining what is important to your work and job. This strategy also helps you identify how your work affects others and how other people's work could affect you.

The fundamental premise of LO-PEMEO is to *ask questions*. By asking yourself questions, you maintain your alertness. By seeking answers, you continually learn and become more adaptable and effective in the workplace. The big question is: *What questions should I ask?* The questions identified in LO-PEMEO help you to ask many of the right questions. The Job Aid at the end of this book lists the key questions this book addresses.

Apply the strategies: There is a learning activity after each thinking strategy to help you apply the strategy to your work.

Workplace examples are used throughout this book. Some examples may not fit your type of work or workplace. In such cases, think of your own examples to increase your understanding of the thinking strategies.

There are many excellent books on critical thinking. One useful resource for information on critical thinking is *The Foundation of Critical Thinking*. A large amount of information relating to thinking can be viewed and printed from its website at www.criticalthinking.org.

MetaThink™

Apply a Business Process Thinking Strategy

This generic thinking strategy has three major steps:
- **Discover**
- **Decide**
- **Deliver**

The success of the business process thinking strategy depends on two additional measures:
- confirming expectations
- determining satisfaction

Confirming expectations and determining satisfaction are important to having satisfied customers and minimizing rework. These two factors are built into the business process.

This business process is useful when working with both internal and external customers; it is particularly useful for establishing goals and expectations. The business process can also be used as part of a problem-solving process to determine or select a response to a problem. Solving problems is dealt with in detail in the book *JobThink*.

The business process described in this book provides the basis for more sophisticated communication processes tailored for people in different occupations. For example:

- sales personnel
- consultants
- nurses
- doctors
- accountants
- counselors
- managers
- team leaders
- foremen

NOTE In this book, the term *customer* is used broadly and includes your peers, your supervisor, and people from other departments (i.e., internal customers).

The three steps of the business process thinking strategy (discover, decide, and deliver) can be applied to specific tasks, job assignments, and large projects. For large work assignments, you can apply the business process to various stages of the work. Using this basic business process regularly can help you be more successful in your job and, at the same time, reduce the risk of losses due to rework.

2.1 Discover

The discover step involves exploring to determine *what is important* to your customer regarding a product or service. This information helps you select a shortlist of practical options for making a decision. Making a decision can be difficult when there are a lot of options to choose from. It is easier to make a decision as to which option is best at meeting the customer's expectations using a short list rather than a long list of options.

Let's say you want to buy a vehicle and you have many choices. You may not be aware of all the options or sure of what would be your best purchase. You go to a sales person for advice on the assumption that he or she is knowledgeable about vehicles and can help you make a choice. The sales person provides leadership by asking specific questions to determine your needs, wants, likes, dislikes, and price range.

Your needs, wants, expectations, and price range are the criteria you use for making a decision about which car to buy. Criteria for *products* often include the product specifications (e.g., function, application, size, color), costs, and possibly delivery time and location.

After you answer the sales person's questions, the sales person *confirms* his or her understanding by summarizing your comments.

In the preceding example, the sales person:

- provides leadership to help you think about issues that are important to you and must be considered when making a decision.
- presents criteria that will help you make a decision in your best interest. Criteria used for decision-making are different for different circumstances. For instance, determining the best way to do a specific job would include criteria such as safety, environment, efficiency, quality, available resources, and cost.
- confirms his or her understanding of your position about the key issues. Confirming understanding has several benefits:
  - If you agree with the feedback, your confidence or trust in the sales person increases because he or she demonstrated an understanding of you and the issues.
  - If the sales person misunderstood your needs, you can make the correction.
  - You can expand on an issue or add to the list of issues that must be considered when making the purchase.
  - The sales person now has information that helps him or her narrow down options to those items that may be of interest to you.

The sales person must communicate effectively to provide quality feedback to you. Two ways are:

- Express the desire to understand you:
  - *I really want to understand your interests so that I can make useful recommendations.*

— I would like to confirm my understanding of your concerns so that I can make suggestions as to what will work for you.

- Paraphrase what you have just said. Paraphrasing is summarizing what has been said; it is not parroting or repeating what has been said (which can become very aggravating):
  - A sales person might say, *So you're saying that you like...*
  - A person receiving direction from a supervisor might say, *You want me to...* or *So the... needs to be...*

NOTE *SafeThink* training is also delivered as a course. The *SafeThink Coach-the-Coach* course provides participants with opportunities to practice several different communication styles, including paraphrasing.

In the previous example, a product is used to explain applying the *discover* process to identify criteria for making a decision. The discover process applies equally well to tasks. Criteria for tasks address what has to be done, how it has to be done, and how well it has to be done. Specific criteria for tasks could include:

- what has to be done
- who will do the work
- where the work will be done
- what conditions affect doing the work or timing of the work
- what materials will be used
- what tools and equipment will be used
- how the task will be done
- what quality of work is expected (i.e., how well the task will be done)

LEARNING ACTIVITY 1

Business Process: Discover Step

This learning activity will help you refine your thinking skills to identify what is important to customers and the criteria they use to make decisions and determine their satisfaction with a service or product.

Write legibly: you will use your notes for question 9.

1. Identify a service or product that you bought in the past that you were not satisfied with.

    _____

2. Check the reasons for your dissatisfaction.

    ☐ the sales person didn't understand my needs and expectations

    ☐ the sales person didn't give me viable options

    ☐ the company did not deliver on its promises

3. Identify a service or product you were very satisfied with.

    _____

4. Check the reasons for your satisfaction.

    ☐ the sales person asked questions to find out my needs, wants, and expectations

    ☐ the sales person communicated his/her understanding of my needs, wants, and expectations

    ☐ the sales person gave me viable options

    ☐ the sales person confirmed my decision

    ☐ the company delivered on its promises

    ☐ the company followed up to ensure I was a satisfied customer

5. Identify a goal that has more than one option for making a decision (e.g., buying a vehicle, selecting a vacation destination, replacing the siding on your house, or arranging for a service that can be done in a variety of ways).

    My goal is _____

    _____

6. For the goal you identified in question 5, list six criteria that are important to making a decision (e.g., cost, sequence of work, resources, time, function, color, size).

_____

_____

_____

_____

_____

_____

7. When selecting an option, certain criteria must be met while others may not be as critical. For example, safety must be ensured—an option that cannot ensure personnel safety is not acceptable. From your list of criteria in question 6, identify one criterion that must be met when deciding which option is the best choice.

_____

8. Often the criteria for decision-making are not all equal in importance. Putting the criteria in sequence from most important to least important can make it easier for you to choose from several options. Using the list of criteria you identified in question 6, remove the must be met criterion you identified in question 7. Then sequence the remaining criteria from most important to least important.

_____

_____

_____

_____

_____

_____

9. The instructions up to now have focused on you as a customer. Now you will help a customer. Using your partner's notes, ask questions to determine his/

her expectations. You can also ask questions that are not addressed in the notes. You may want to put the answers on a separate sheet of paper. Summarize your findings by giving your partner feedback about his or her expectations.

2.2 Decide

Understanding and *confirming* your customer's needs, wants, concerns, and issues (i.e., the *discover* step) helps you make better recommendations to your customer. Your goal is to meet your customer's expectations and have a satisfied customer.

Continuing with the sales person example, having completed the *discover* step, the sales person can now make practical recommendations that will help you reach a decision. Often this *decide* step can be collaborative in that the sales person may ask you if you have a specific purchase in mind. The sales person could offer several options, explaining the pros and cons for your particular needs or uses. Alternatively, he or she could offer one general suggestion (e.g., a category or type of item such as a van versus a truck) and confirm if that suggestion would meet your needs. If the answer is yes, the sales person could then provide several options within that category.

All options address the *must* criteria as well as several of the other criteria identified in the *discover* step. You then have to determine which option best meets your decision-making criteria. The sales person may help you by pointing out how the features of each option meet or do not meet your criteria. If the sales person is able to offer you one or more vehicles that meet your expectations, you probably will make a selection and purchase a specific vehicle.

It is possible that sometimes you could make a decision to purchase a product (not necessarily a vehicle) that has negative implications for you or others. The sales person must decide whether to deal with the issue and, if action is required, determine how strong a stance to take. For example, if you were building a deck onto your house and you had undersized the cross members, the sales person should point out that the deck would be spongy and sag after a few years. The sales person should also give you suggestions on how to better support the deck.

If you made a selection that could create a safety issue, the sales person should take a strong stance and suggest the best alternative. For example, if you selected an undersized hook for a winch cable, the hook could break, putting you or others at risk of an impact injury. The sales person should take a strong stance and recommend the correct size of hook.

After you have made a decision, it is important for the sales person to confirm your decision in case there is any possibility of a misunderstanding. The sales person would reflect back to you the specifications of a product. For a task, the sales person would state the specifics about what has to be done, how it has to be done, and how well it has to be done.

NOTE

The book *WorkThink* provides opportunities to clearly define tasks and effectively communicate expectations for performing the tasks.

For large job assignments, the job may be divided into smaller parts and a decision made on how to go about doing each part.

When working on specific parts of a project, always keep in mind the big picture, including the purpose and goals of the project as a whole. Sometimes the decision-making process for specific parts of the job assignment becomes more difficult when other job assignments must also be addressed. Issues such as having limited resources and the need to coordinate the work with other work may have to be considered. To carry out specific work, the business process is a very useful tool to ensure that:

• the customer's expectations are understood

- the customer confirms what he/she wants and is willing to pay for. Work results from this decision.
- the work is performed in a way that minimizes interference with other work assignments
- the services and products meet the customer's expectation.

When an HDC consultant interviews a Subject Matter Expert (SME) to gather content for a technical training program, the consultant often combines the *discover* and *decide* steps. For example, the consultant:

- starts with the discover step by getting agreement on criteria for determining the content for training (and content that should not be included). Getting the SME's agreement about the selection criteria makes the process of deciding what content belongs in the training and what doesn't belong more objective (i.e., reduces the potential of conflict between consultant and SME and contributes to ensuring the training is relevant and useful).
- gets agreement on whether the training focuses on skills, knowledge, or both. The consultant confirms the decision with the SME by discussing the methods that will be used to assess the trainee.
- asks the SME to provide an overview of the task and/or technology. The consultant then summarizes the SME's input by suggesting how the knowledge could be organized into sections or the task divided into parts. The consultant confirms the organization/structure with the SME by asking: *If we divide this... into these parts, will it meet your needs? Does it fit the job?* In this part of the interview, the consultant has combined the *discover* and *decide* steps.
- the consultant then continues to combine the *discover* and *decide* steps by using a directed interviewing process to gather the content from the SME. Every few minutes, the consultant confirms the accuracy and completeness of the content that is being gathered.

Sometimes the decision-making process can be complex and difficult. The book *JobThink* provides training on using a decision-making matrix to rate options in response to problems.

LEARNING ACTIVITY 2

Business Process: Decide Step

This learning activity will help you refine your ability to work with customers to help them decide on the best course of action to meet their wants or needs.

1. Using the goal and decision-making criteria you stated in Learning Activity 1 (questions 5 and 6), identify two options that could meet your expectations.

    Option 1: _____

    Option 2: _____

2. Using the decision-making criteria you stated in Learning Activity 1, select the option that would best meet your expectations. Specify how that option satisfies the criteria better than the other option.

    The option that best meets my expectations is _____

    I selected this option because _____

    _____

    _____

    _____

    _____

3. Give an example where your customer hypothetically makes a poor decision. Would you point out your concern and, if so, how strong a stance would you take?

    Example of a customer's poor decision: _____

    _____

    I would take a _____ *stance to let the customer know that the decision was a poor one.*

2.3 Deliver

The *deliver* step of the business process involves:
- efficiently delivering the services and products that the customer wants (and is willing to pay for in the case of external customers and possibly some internal customers)
- confirming customer expectations
- determining customer satisfaction

Ensuring Customer Satisfaction

As part of its business system, your organization has developed processes, practices, procedures, standards, and controls to ensure that customers are satisfied. The processes and procedures may be modified for specific clients; however, the goals remain the same:
- plan, control, and track production and services
- work efficiently (optimization)
- minimize rework (control losses)
- maintain quality assurance (the customer's and your organization's expectations)
- communicate effectively with the customer

When customers are dissatisfied because of poor services or products or because the wrong products were provided, many organizations acknowledge the problem and promptly correct the problem at no cost to the customer. Acknowledging fault for customer dissatisfaction requires staff to accept responsibility for the problem and make corrections. It is very important for organizational success that staff:
- acknowledge the deficiency or problem
- correct the problem
- find ways to reduce the probability of the problem occurring again, and then
- move forward (instead of fretting over what happened in the past)

For the organization to remain competitive, all staff must be accountable for their successes and failures and continually strive to improve.

Customer satisfaction research indicates that customer trust increases significantly if, after a problem occurred, the organization corrected the problem promptly to the customer's satisfaction.

If, during the course of delivering services and products, there are circumstances that could cause customer dissatisfaction and a subsequent loss to your organization, you must apply the business process. Start with the discover step to ensure that the customer's concerns and expectations are understood. Then, after you understand the customer's concerns and expectations, take action to ensure customer satisfaction.

Confirming Customer Expectations

If you have doubts about understanding or meeting the customer's expectations, you must clarify expectations. You may also have to adjust the services or products that you are delivering. The customer may have to be contacted for clarification and input. Seek advice from your co-workers and/or supervisor. You might be concerned that asking for input and clarification from others may imply shortcomings in your original work or competence. However, professionalism and the need to act in your organization's best interest demands that this communication occur promptly. When contacting the customer, one way to break the ice is to tell the customer that you really want to meet his or her expectations and need some clarification. For example: *I/we really want to meet your expectations and need clarification about ... .*

Most customers are pleased to know that you are genuinely concerned about meeting their expectations and are willing to provide additional input to ensure their expectations are met. After you get the customer's input, you must confirm his or her expectations and then take action to meet those expectations (discover, decide, deliver).

If you are confirming expectations in writing, consider the amount of detail that person wants. Generally, less detail is required by people who are higher in the organization. However, in addition to providing a summary, you may have to give that person the option to read the detail.

Sometimes you may identify an issue that has negative implications for the customer. You have to decide whether to deal with the issue or not and, if action is required, determine how strong a stance to take with the customer. Unless there is a breach of ethics or legislation, the customer usually makes the final decision.

It is important that customers keep a positive image of you and your organization. The key is communication so that the customer knows that your organization is demonstrating its commitment to having a satisfied customer.

You may have opportunities to communicate concerns about costs, quality, and customer satisfaction as a demonstration of your commitment to customer satisfaction. For example:

- confirming customer expectations
- discussing costs of alternate ways of dealing with an issue
- suggesting ways to reduce costs, add value, or enhance the quality of products
- when you have doubts about meeting the customer's expectations, taking the initiative to address the concerns, often through discussion with co-workers and the customer
- asking the customer about their satisfaction with a service or product.

NOTE If you ask for feedback from the customer after you have provided the service, use caution when interpreting the feedback. To avoid offending you, a somewhat dissatisfied customer may not be frank and forthright.

Sometimes, you may have to get clarification to ensure that the customer's expectations are being met. In some cases, the customers initiate the need for clarification because they want to make changes. In other cases, you may not be totally confident that you understand the customer's expectations. After getting clarification, you must get the customer to confirm the expectations to prevent any misunderstandings.

For internal customers, a verbal confirmation is usually done. For external customers, preparing a written summary may be prudent.

Document the agreement, including the date, persons involved, and recommended decisions. If, in the future, the customer questions the services or products, you can justify the actions taken.

You can get customer confirmation by:
- verbally summarizing information and getting the customer to verbally agree/approve
- summarizing the customer's request.

Summarizing and getting the customer's approval is a good method when there is a lot of information. To introduce the summary statements, you may communicate your commitment to meeting the customer's expectations.

The customer then must agree with you or clarify the expectations. If there are changes, consider reflecting what the customer says; reflecting is a good way to confirm the customer's expectations. Reflecting involves paraphrasing or summarizing the customer's statements. For example:

To a supervisor: *So you're saying that I can only use the model 24 grinder to deglaze the surface.*

To a buyer: *So you want to change the siding color to avocado green.*

Generally, when discussing issues with the customer, paraphrasing is better than repeating the customer's statements because paraphrasing demonstrates understanding of the key issues. When documenting information, repeating the customer's statements may be more appropriate than paraphrasing. Make sure the customer responds to the statement(s) with a yes, no, or further clarification. In some cases, instead of responding to the statement, the customer may change topics or go into detail. You then will have to backtrack and get the customer to agree to the original statement.

Determining Customer Satisfaction

Applying the business process does not guarantee customer satisfaction. Circumstances both within and outside of your control, or changing customer expectations, may cause customer dissatisfaction. To reduce the potential of having a dissatisfied customer, you could confirm customer expectations at every major step in delivering the service and/or products. In doing so, you ensure customer satisfaction and reduce the risk of losses. Of course, you need to use the confirmation strategy with some reservation; you could over do it and aggravate the customer.

As a rule, customers do not voluntarily express their level of satisfaction with the services and products that are delivered. Customers take for granted that the services and products should be good because that's what they have been promised and that's what they are paying for. Usually customers do not complain about a service or product unless they are very dissatisfied. At that point, your and/or your organization's reputation could be damaged and corrective action could be costly.

In addition to your efforts to ensure customer satisfaction, your organization may also have a formal process to get customer feedback. After the service or product has been delivered, the customer is contacted either by phone, e-mail, or letter to get feedback. Unfortunately, not all organizations follow up with the customer after the customer expresses dissatisfaction.

NOTE

In the workplace, you informally may receive day-to-day feedback about your performance. If you don't get the feedback you need to improve your performance, you should ask co-workers and your boss. Many organizations also have formal performance reviews where you receive feedback about your performance. Unfortunately, when formal performance reviews are infrequent, you have fewer opportunities to adjust your performance to meet expectations of the job. The feedback may also be too late to fix a problem.

At the completion of a large project, some organizations have a project review meeting (debriefing). The staff celebrate the successes, identify areas of difficulty, and determine ways to make future projects more successful.

On your own, you may have opportunities to check with customers six or more months after delivery to see how well your work or product stands up over time. The feedback you receive can be very useful in learning ways to improve your work and help you make better decisions to improve customer satisfaction. This long-term feedback can make the difference in you being a *satisfactory* performer or an *exemplary* performer.

If you don't receive long-term feedback, you will continue doing what you have always done; you may never learn what worked well and what didn't. The fact that you show interest in contacting the customer also contributes to customer satisfaction.

LEARNING ACTIVITY 3

Business Process: Deliver Step

This learning activity will help you better understand your organization's systems, processes, policies, and standards to ensure satisfied customers.

1. Give an example where someone provided excellent service only to find out that the service wasn't what the customer wanted.

   _____

   _____

2. Give an example when, in the middle of providing a service and/or product, you had doubts about the customer's expectations. Did you ask for confirmation or clarification that resulted in changes?

   _____

   _____

   _____

   _____

3. Give an example when, in the middle of providing a service and/or product, your customer wanted to make changes. Did your organization have a formal change process for dealing with the customer? If yes, explain the process. If no, explain how you would apply the business process to ensure customer satisfaction.

_____

_____

_____

_____

4. What are your organization's policies and procedures for handling customer complaints (internal and external customers)?

_____

_____

_____

5. What formal process does your organization use to follow up after providing services and/or products to determine the level of customer satisfaction?

_____

_____

_____

_____

6. In your opinion, how important is it to your organization to have satisfied customers (internal and external customers)? Support your answer.

_____

_____

_____

_____

_____

7. Give an example where you can use the business process in your workplace (e.g., with co-worker, supervisor, team leader, another department).

_____

_____

_____

_____

2.4 Summary of the Business Process

The three major steps to the business process are:
- **discover:** Provide leadership to determine the criteria that the customer will use to reach a decision. Confirm your understanding of the criteria to your customer.
- **decide:** Give the customer one or more choices. Help the customer determine the choice that best meets his or her decision-making criteria. Confirm the customer's decision.
- **deliver:** Give the customer what they want and are willing to pay for (if an external customer). Confirm with the customer their expectations and satisfaction during and after delivery of the product or service.

Although the business process is essential for achieving customer satisfaction, it is not sufficient to ensure a satisfied customer. For any situation, the factors associated with that situation must be considered. For example, to effectively help a buyer select a vehicle that he or she will be satisfied with, the salesperson must provide leadership by identifying and defining the factors associated with vehicles, transportation, operating costs, and customer preferences. Sometimes, you may not know what factors are important to your customer. To provide leadership, you can use the business process (plus other strategies such as using corporate goals) to understand your customer's concerns. If you don't know what factors affect the customer's decision-making, you could ask. For example: _What is most important to you about... (the service or product)?_

Always confirm your understanding of your customer's expectations, decisions, and satisfaction with the product or service.

Viewing and treating your supervisor and other work groups as customers can help you to direct your work efforts in ways that others appreciate.

MetaThink™

Use Corporate Goals

The book *JobThink* emphasizes the value of using corporate goals to select solutions to problems. Corporate goals help you determine what is important to your organization. Corporate goals are also used when applying other thinking strategies addressed in this book. For example, corporate goals help you to understand your internal customers, their concerns, and their expectations.

Below is a list of corporate goals common to many organizations. Technically, the corporate goals should be further explained in terms of outcomes (e.g., maintain a healthy and safe workplace).In this book, for convenience, only the areas of concern are listed.

Corporate Goals	
• health and safety	• minimizing losses
• environment	• controlling costs
• regulatory compliance	• customer satisfaction
• corporate policies	• public image
• equipment optimization	• public disruption
• equipment life and reliability	• teamwork
• energy consumption	• communication
• material optimization	• decision-making

Within an organization, the corporate goals do not apply equally between departments and each department may have different priorities. For your personal use, you need to refine the list. You should also place the corporate goals in priority with the understanding that priorities can change with changing circumstances.

Use corporate goals

This learning activity will help determine the issues that are important to your job so you can better focus your efforts and make decisions in the best interests of your organization.

1. Using the list of corporate goals, make a short list of goals that apply to your job. You may add corporate goals specific to your organization and/or reword the goals to suit your job. Number the corporate goals from highest priority to lowest priority.

   _____

   _____

   _____

   _____

   _____

Assess Issues from Different Job Perspectives

It can be difficult for you to determine the issues and concerns that are important at the corporate, job, and employee levels. One thinking process for identifying performance-related issues at each of these levels is to put yourself in the position of those who represent the various levels.

Upper Management—Upper management represents the organization and is responsible for achieving business success, which often includes satisfying the financial expectations of shareholders. Operationally, management must ensure that business assets are used effectively and losses kept to a practical minimum. Upper management identifies strategic business objectives or corporate goals to provide direction to operations staff about what is important. These goals are often further refined at the departmental level.

Departmental-Level Supervisors—At the departmental level, the supervisor or team leader represents management and is responsible for ensuring that specific assets are used effectively to achieve productivity targets. Planning, coordinating, and controlling work activities are important roles for supervisors and team leaders.

Ensuring employees work safely, efficiently, effectively, and in the way the organization wants to do business is a major objective. Since people in these positions represent management, issues relating to organizational goals and performance benchmarks are always of concern to them.

Employee level—Employees often have concerns about keeping their jobs and/or being promoted. Compensation and job satisfaction are important. Employees recognize that working safely, efficiently, and to the supervisor's, team's, or customer's satisfaction is important to achieving their personal goals. Employees may struggle to determine what the work expectations are, especially if their learning is isolated to doing their jobs without an understanding of the overall business.

Supervisor's Concerns

For job success, one of the most important positions to understand is that of your boss (who may be a manager, supervisor, or team leader). These people are at a level between upper management and front line or floor employees. Being in the middle, your supervisor has the challenge of meeting both management and employee expectations which, at times, may conflict. He or she represents management and is responsible for achieving specific productivity goals for that department. He or she must also find ways to motivate employees and maintain morale, even while reinforcing policies that potentially upset employees.

The supervisor's job is to achieve department productivity goals by using the resources available to the department (money, equipment, materials, and people). If the supervisor is successful at achieving the department's goals, he or she may be rewarded for good performance. Conversely, if the supervisor fails to achieve the goals, he or she will be pressed by upper management to do better.

To understand the types of concern a supervisor may have, imagine that you are a supervisor on your first day on the job in a new type of organization. You probably would have many general questions about the business such as:

- What does this department do or produce?
- Who are the customers?
- What are the productivity goals for this department?
- What is the budget for this department?
- What goals is the department achieving? Not achieving?
- What are the department's competitive strategies?
- What are my roles and responsibilities?
- How will my performance be assessed?
- What authority do I have to take action or make changes?
- What are the general technical or work processes?
- What is the general quality of the equipment, materials, and people?
- Is the workforce stable? What size is the workforce?
- What was the previous supervisor's management style?
- What are the different job positions and how do they relate to each other?
- What is the level of morale of the department and of employees?
- What are the critical issues affecting productivity?
- Are there any critical safety, health, environmental, or other regulatory issues affecting this department?

Over the next few weeks as supervisor, you would have more specific questions, such as:

- Are customers (internal and external) satisfied with the quality of the department's services and products?
- Is the equipment being used effectively, efficiently, and in a way that extends equipment life?
- Is the quality of materials satisfactory for work efficiency and for achieving quality results?
- Can material waste be reduced?
- Are people being employed effectively to achieve productivity goals?
- How does each job position specifically affect other job positions?
- What are the roles and responsibilities of each job position?
- What tasks are performed in each job position?
- Do employees know what is expected of them?

- Do employees have the necessary resources to be effective at carrying out their work?
- What is the quality of performance of each employee?
- How do I directly or indirectly measure people's performance for each task?
- What are the incentives and rewards for excellent performance?
- What should be the limits of authority for each job position and task?
- What are the policies affecting department and employee performance?
- What would be the reaction of employees, upper management, and the union if I assigned work that is outside existing job descriptions?
- Are there ways of improving production and the quality of services and products without increasing costs?
- Is the budget adequate for equipment upgrades and for developing staff?
- Do I have the authority to make changes?

The answers to these questions help to describe a department and identify some of the issues important to supervisors. To understand your supervisor and help him or her use the department's resources effectively, you need to ask and find answers for these types of questions. If you understand what is important to your supervisor and his or her concerns and issues, you can be better at working in ways that contribute to his or her success. In turn, your job satisfaction and personal success will likely improve.

Viewing Issues From Other People's Perspectives

In your workplace, you also need to be able to view issues from the perspective of other people, such as those who affect you doing your work, those who are impacted by your work, and external customers. Often, when you need to understand a person's perspective, you don't have a list such as the one above to provide guidance. To successfully view issues from a different person's perspective, pretend to be that person with their education, experiences, skills, beliefs, values, and personal attributes. The saying, *You have to walk a mile in the other person's shoes to understand their situation* has a lot of merit. It may not, however, be sufficient to understand that person's concerns and issues and can be cause for misunderstandings. Your experiences, skills, and abilities may be different from that person's. That person may be more or less capable than you are in dealing with the situation. Supervisors may have more or less supervisory training than you do. Employees new to the position may have more or less work experience than you do and their education may be quite different. Your way of mentally processing information and your preferred style of learning may be different from others. Communication methods that suit you may not suit others. For you to effectively put yourself *in other people's shoes* to understand what is important to them, their issues, concerns, and capabilities, you have to imagine yourself having the education, experiences, skills, and personal attributes of those specific people. Ask yourself, *If I were that person, how would I view the issue?* Viewing issues from the other person's perspective is very helpful when resolving conflicts and negotiating win-win agreements.

MetaThink™

Assess issues from different job perspectives

This learning activity will help you better understand the concerns others may have and the reasons for their actions.

1. List four responsibilities of your supervisor.

    _____

    _____

    _____

    _____

2. For each item below, do you feel your supervisor has adequate resources to achieve the department's goals?

    equipment: _____

    materials: _____

    money (budget): _____

    people: _____

3. What do you think are your supervisor's challenges and concerns regarding each item listed below?

    delegating work: _____

    _____

    planning work: _____

    _____

    coordinating work: _____

    _____

    controlling work: _____

    _____

    providing performance feedback: _____

    _____

4.   Think of someone that is in a different job position or department that can negatively affect your work. Put yourself in that person's position and try to determine the reasons or causes for that person's actions. From that person's perspective, why do you think they do not take action to reduce the negative impact on your work?

_____

_____

_____

_____

5.   State what would be important to and what would be an issue for the positions listed below.

manager of a clothing store: _____

_____

_____

sales person in the same clothing store: _____

_____

_____

_____

coach of a sports team: _____

_____

_____

player on the same team: _____

_____

_____

MetaThink™

36

Section 5

Use Variables

Your organization hired you to contribute to its business goals. Your job, however, dictates and restricts what you can and cannot do to be productive. Your job description defines and limits your authority to make decisions. You often have to work with specific equipment, materials, co-workers, and customers. Given specific resources and defined authority to make decisions, you must learn to work in ways that contribute to business success. To be effective in your job, you need to know:

- what you have to work with, such as specific equipment and materials
- what you can and cannot control
- what you must respond to and how to respond
- the expected results you must achieve through your effort of carrying out work

This information can be expressed in terms of variables. Two definitions of variables apply to the workplace:

1) *A variable is that which is prone to change or has the potential to change, especially in quantity and quality.*

   Examples: outdoor temperature, number of customers, rpm of an engine, flow rate of oil from an oil well

2) *A variable is that which has a specific value in relation to a set of values.*

   Examples: composition of ore from a specific vein in a mine, maximum operating pressure of a pipe, flow rate of a positive displacement pump

According to the prveious definitions, variables can be either *static* or *dynamic*.

Static Variables

Static (fixed) variables are variables which cannot be easily changed. For example, the rated power of a gasoline engine is static; with considerable effort and costs, however, a mechanic can modify the engine to increase its power. The volume (quantity) of gas going through a compressor is static. However, some compressors are designed so that a mechanic, with some effort, can change the volume of gas being compressed. The size of tools and equipment is static. You may or may not be able to select the size that is most suitable for a specific application.

In some cases, a static or steady state is desirable. For example, a gas plant may have two boilers providing steam to the entire plant. One boiler may be chosen to provide the base load (steady state) while the load on the other boiler varies according to demand.

Dynamic Variables

Dynamic variables are prone to change. For example, the rpm of a gasoline engine in an automobile may change regularly.

In a gas plant, process temperatures and pressures are prone to change. When it is desirable that these pressures and temperatures remain constant, you may have to make adjustments to maintain the desired setpoints.

Controllable and Non-Controllable Variables

Static and dynamic variables can also be controllable or non-controllable. You may or may not have control over a variable, be it static or dynamic. If you do not have control, you may have to adjust the way you work to accommodate or work around the issue. If the variable can be controlled and you have authority to take action, you must know how and under what conditions to make the adjustments.

NOTE

Whether a variable is controllable or non-controllable depends to some degree on the circumstances. For example:

- an air compressor's design determines the compressor's maximum operating pressure; workers can make pressure adjustments up to the stated maximum pressure.
- a supervisor may have control of the type of tools and equipment used for a specific job.
- workers may not have control over the type of tools and equipment that they must use to do a specific job.

NOTE

Sometimes the work environment dictates the tools that **cannot** be used. For example:
- earth moving equipment may not be able to access a back yard where re-landscaping needs to be done.
- an engineered board manufacturer may have to adjust both product quality and product dimensions to satisfy different customers. In this case, workers do not have control over product standards but can adjust equipment variables to achieve the standards.

The two categories of variables—static/dynamic and controllable/non-controllable—combine to produce four possible types of variable as shown in the following chart:

Variable	Static	Dynamic
Controllable	Static (fixed) and Controllable Variable	Dynamic and Controllable Variable
Non-Controllable	Static (fixed) and Non-Controllable Variable	Dynamic and Non-Controllable Variable

For any job position you may hold, identifying and classifying the variables that affect your work is an excellent thinking strategy for identifying what is important to your job, your work, and your performance. The critical issue is to identify the *right* variables—the variables relating to your job. For example:
- An equipment operator may not have any concern about the thickness of metal used for a vessel or a structural

support, but a welder may need to know the exact thickness and composition of the metal, the physical forces on the metal, the thermal expansion the metal experiences during use, and the environment to which the metal is exposed.

- A mechanic may not be concerned about the operating pressures of a pump but an operator may need to know the minimum, maximum, and optimal suction and discharge pressures.

PEMEO:
- *People*
- *Equipment*
- *Materials*
- *Environment*
- *Organization*

Most tasks result in making a *change* such as filling out a spreadsheet, installing a guard rail, or delivering mail. The goal of some tasks is to keep equipment at a steady state so that changes are consistent (e.g., process equipment in the petro-chemical industry). To determine which variables are important for your job, you need to assess your tasks to determine how the work affects PEMEO and how PEMEO affects the work. Using PEMEO to identify variables that are important to your job is a practical thinking strategy because most issues important to corporate, job, and employee performance involve PEMEO.

Identify Work-Related Variables

To identify work-related variables, use the following steps. However, the order in which you carry out the steps may change, depending on the work context (e.g., processes, manufacturing, fabrication, construction, quality control). As you read the steps, mark off the concepts that apply to your job and work environment.

- **Identify the tasks and desired results for a specific job position.** Results are often measured in terms of quality, quantity, time, and timeliness. The units of measurement for results define some of the variables that are important to that job. Examine the actions you perform to do the tasks. You are either making changes to variables or monitoring variables to determine their status.

- **Identify the materials, tools, and equipment** you need and determine the most efficient sequence for completing the job. Consider the variables that define the quality of results. Identify variables affecting the efficiency and effectiveness of carrying out the task (e.g., size of tools and equipment, ambient temperature, expected quality of results of carrying out one or more steps). The order and/or number of steps to complete a task may change as a result of a change in variables. For example, if the temperature of a product used to coat concrete is below 10°C, the product must be warmed so that the product can be applied effectively. If a step of a task results in a change in conditions (e.g., an electric motor starts), the impact that the step has on PEMEO must be assessed. You may have to change the order of the steps or add steps to ensure co-workers are not adversely affected.

- **Consider the primary function and operating specifications of tools and equipment.** For example:
  - **function, size, and type of equipment.** These variables affect selection, application, operation, and maintenance (e.g., function may affect the application or use of tools and equipment; size affects efficiency and effectiveness of work; and type affects the quality of results, operating procedures, and maintenance requirements).
  - **operation specifications** (e.g., minimum, maximum, and optimum fluid pressure and temperature for a pump; minimum, maximum, and optimum rpm of a compressor; maximum load for a truck; maximum cutting depth of a portable power saw)
  - **reliability specifications** (e.g., variables for rotating equipment may include vibration, rpm, and lubrication and coolant temperatures, pressures, and flow rates)
  - **efficiency specifications** (e.g., operating specifications to minimize energy consumption)
  - **effectiveness specifications** (e.g., depth of cut and cutting speed of a milling tool)
  - When selecting components for equipment repair, **identify the specifications for equipment, application, installation, and removal.** Often, selecting the required component involves variables associated with fit and function of the component. The specific application of the equipment can also affect

component selection. For example, the grade of a sanding belt depends on whether the sanding is done for shaping or finishing. The environment to which the component is exposed can also affect component selection; for example, a pump used to transfer caustic products requires seals that are made of a material that does not corrode in the presence of the caustic substance. Often components are replaced *in kind* (same specifications) provided the original component functions well, is reliable, and has an acceptable life span. Often a component must be installed in a particular way and to manufacturer's specifications (variables). For example, bolts for many components must be torqued (tightened) a specific amount.

- **Assess the materials used** to determine the variables that are being affected (e.g., size, shape). Determine the specifications (composition, properties, characteristics) that you have to pay attention to or work with:
  - specifications of materials entering equipment
  - specifications of materials leaving equipment (desired results)
  - specifications of semi-finished materials used for fabrication or construction
  - specifications of materials after they have been fitted and attached
  - specifications of materials that have been modified (e.g., grade of road; size, shape, and location of an excavation for a building foundation)
- **Identify materials added to, removed from, or modified in the environment.** Consider ways to reduce consumption and energy use.
- **Identify agents that can cause harm.** With the understanding of the task, tools, equipment, and materials, assess your work environment and the actions you take to perform the task. Determine if there are any actions, conditions, or events that can expose you to agents of cause that can harm you. The *SafeThink* book focuses on using a structured critical thinking strategy to identify and predict hazardous situations.
- **Identify the variables affecting the corporate goals** (e.g., number of customers, customer expectations, costs

to repair versus replace, budgets, policies). Time to do the work and timing of the work can affect the work performed by others doing the same job or other jobs.
- Ask your co-workers or supervisor to **identify the critical issues when performing the tasks.** The answers will most likely be general statements about loss and optimization of PEMEO or the identification of specific variables associated with PEMEO.

NOTE In the above examples, safety and working effectively and efficiently were items towards the end of the list of steps. (However, many organizations like to list safety first as a priority.) Sometimes a clear understanding about the task, tools, equipment, and materials is required to be able to identify issues affecting safety and job performance.

For each variable, determine if the variable is static or dynamic and controllable or non-controllable (for your job position). Determine if you must react to the variable or affect the variable. For example:
- when the composition of a raw material changes, you may need to adjust equipment to accommodate the change
- when the operating temperature of a piece of equipment increases, you may need to make adjustments to the equipment, technical processes, materials, or work processes to reduce the temperature
- if the vibration of a piece of equipment increases, you may need to shut down the equipment before further damage occurs.

To correct the problem, rotating parts may have to be balanced and/or worn components replaced.

The previous list of work-related variables is complex because many different types of work and work environments are considered. However, the number of variables is limited for a given task, desired quality of results, and specific work environment. Through elimination, the number of variables can be further reduced. For example, a specific task and workplace may not expose you to current electricity (an agent of cause).

Focusing on variables is an effective way to determine what is important to you, your supervisor, and the company when you do work. To give meaning to the variables, consider the impact the variables have on PEMEO. The impact of a variable can often be put into one of two categories: loss or optimization (LO). To strategically focus your thinking, for each given variable, consider LO-PEMEO.

NOTE

The books listed in the introduction address the domains of PEMEO. Each book emphasizes *asking the right questions* as a strategy to identify what is important to employee, job, and corporate performance. Within each book, loss and/or optimization (LO) are the main themes, hence the word LO-PEMEO.

The LO-PEMEO thinking strategy requires you to examine five domains (PEMEO) to determine if there is any potential for loss (L) or opportunity for optimization (O) of a work condition, action, or event.

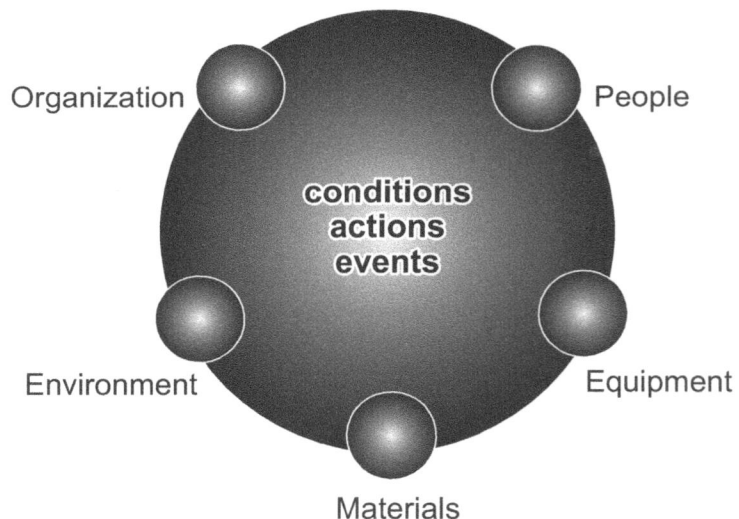

To use the strategy, ask specific questions—but a limited number—for each domain to determine the consequences of the condition, action, or event. If you think the questions

(continued)

are relevant, and you do not have the answers, ask others to obtain the answers. Generally, if a condition, action, or event affects one domain, then other domains are also affected. For example, an employee is using a caustic chemical. If the chemical spills, the employee is at risk of being harmed. The chemical may also cause harm to equipment, materials, and the environment. Excessive use of the chemical would also create an unnecessary cost to the company.

LOSS					OPTIMIZATION	
Loss:	People	LP	P	OP	Optimization: People
Loss:	Equipment	LE	E	OE	Optimization: Equipment
Loss:	Materials	LM	M	OM	Optimization: Materials
Loss:	Environment	LE	E	OE	Optimization: Environment
Loss:	Organization	LO	O	OO	Optimization: Organization

Note: Although some domains of LO-PEMEO may not appear to be applicable to a situation (e.g., safety in an office environment), you should consider the possibility of the domain applying to the situation to eliminate any doubts.

Here is an example of identifying the work-related variables for a gas plant operator who must monitor and control gas plant processes and communicate the findings and the operational actions.

job position: plant operator for a section of a gas plant

   tasks: monitor aerial cooler, make adjustments, communicate findings, and take corrective action

LO-P: Safety hazards include possible contact with hot equipment, rotating parts, and toxic substances. There are high noise levels and, if a leak occurs, a risk of exposure to a combustible or toxic atmosphere. Daily routine activity provides little opportunity for operators to improve efficiency of doing checks. Providing accurate, timely readings of equipment condition and process variables is important.

Some adjustments to equipment settings (controllable variables) may be required.

LO-E: Equipment variables include fan rpm, fan direction of rotation, louver position, and level of vibration. Adjustments are made to equipment variables (controllable) to maintain product output specifications and equipment efficiency, life, and reliability. In winter, frost buildup on louvers (non-controlled variable) restricts air flow. The frost has to be removed. Equipment downstream of the cooler can be affected if the temperature of the product leaving the cooler is outside of the specified limits (off-spec). Equipment life of downstream equipment could be reduced and may have to be adjusted in response to off-spec product. The efficiency and effectiveness of downstream processes may be reduced if the product from the cooler is off-spec.

LO-M: Process variables include pressure, temperature, and flow rate (dynamic and controllable). Adjustments to the aerial cooler may have to be made to maintain the desired temperature. The quality of product going to the downstream processes can be downgraded if the temperature of the product leaving the cooler is outside of the specified limits.

LO-E: An aerial cooler is a closed system. Therefore there is no release of materials to the environment. However, if a leak occurs, materials will vent to atmosphere, requiring the equipment to be shut down and the leak blocked off.

LO-O: Important input, process, and output variables are those affecting coordination of work, communication, documentation, equipment reliability, product quality, costs, and customer satisfaction (i.e., employees working upstream and downstream of the process). When operating changes are made to the cooler, the operator may be expected to communicate the changes to those who will be affected by the change. Documenting the changes may be important for future reference if problems with the process develop and others have to troubleshoot to find the causes for the problems.

After thinking through the work using LO-PEMEO, the operator now has a comprehensive understanding of the work and related issues. With that knowledge, the operator can now be more effective in carrying out tasks and responding to changes in variables including abnormal or emergency conditions. Further, having gained knowledge about the job, the operator now has a much more limited set of questions to ask him or herself in response to changes affecting the job.

NOTE

Section 7 provides an example of using LO-PEMEO to conduct a loss and optimization analysis of a task (a form of critical task analysis).

For your job, you need to know:
- what variables are important
- whether the variables are static or dynamic
- what variables you can control
- what are the quality criteria regarding the variables
- why you would want to make a change to the variables
- why variables change
- what would be the consequences when one or more variables change
- what should be your response to a change in one or more variables

LEARNING ACTIVITY 6

Use variables

For any job position you may hold, identifying and classifying the variables that affect your work is an excellent thinking strategy for identifying what is important to your job, your work, and your performance. The critical issue is to identify the right variables—the variables relating to your job. This learning activity will help you learn to identify variables important to your job.

1. You are using a countertop model electric blender in the kitchen.

   a. What are the variables associated with using the blender?

   _____

   _____

b. Which of the variables are controllable; which are non-controllable?

_____

_____

c. How can the characteristics of the material being blended vary (e.g., large or small chunks, soft or fibrous material)?

_____

_____

d. How can the specifications of the finished product vary?

_____

_____

e. How can the material input characteristics affect the finished product?

_____

_____

f. What adjustments to variables can you make to achieve the quality results you desire?

_____

_____

g. What can you do to make the blending process efficient?

_____

_____

h. What is the environmentally best way to dispose of waste?

_____

_____

      i. What are the safety hazards associated with the handling, operation, and cleaning of the blender?

_____

_____

2.   Think of a task that involves some type of powered tool, equipment, or appliance. Think through the steps of the task and identify the variables associated with the equipment and materials. Fill out the following chart to identify the work-related variables and their impact on PEMEO.

task: _____

equipment: _____

materials: _____

Themes	Variables and Impact on PEMEO
L-P Loss to People (safety)	
O-P Optimize People's Performance	
LO-E Loss and Optimization of Equipment	
LO-M Loss and Optimization of Materials	
LO-E Loss and Optimization of the Environment	
LO-O Loss and Optimization of the Organization	

Use Reasons, Causes, Effects, and Consequences

One of the main reasons exemplary workers are effective at their jobs is that they continually determine reasons, causes, effects, and consequences before, during, and after completing work. With the understanding that they gain, they can make good decisions and take actions that contribute to business success and minimize losses.

NOTE	The terms *reason* and *cause* are often used as synonyms. However, in this book, these terms have different meanings.

Reasons relate to: rationale, motive, goal, purpose, intent, and by design. In business and work environments, reasons are often business goals, strategic business objectives, corporate objectives, PEMEO, beliefs, values, principles, and concepts. Reasons result in consequences that can be positive or negative for PEMEO.

Causes relate to: failure, not intended happening, and unpredicted event. In business and work environments, causes often result in negative consequences and are frequently initiated by failure or change relating to PEMEO. Examples of causes include: a person fails to electrically lock out the proper equipment, the composition of material changes, equipment components fail, and unpredicted or undesirable events occur, such as freezing rain.

To determine the reasons or causes for a workplace being the way it is and the way people work, you need to ask *Why?* In turn, you need a basic understanding of organizations to direct your thinking to answer the why questions.

There are many models that describe the makeup of organizations. The model described in the *JobThink* book uses five constituents to explain the interrelationship of organizational concepts and the work environment. The following illustration shows the five constituents (mission, technology, tasks, corporate objectives, and management and operational systems):

These five constituents help you focus your efforts in ways that contribute to corporate and job performance. For this section, some key points are taken from the model to explain organizational design in a way that makes it practical to determine reasons, causes, effects, and consequences.

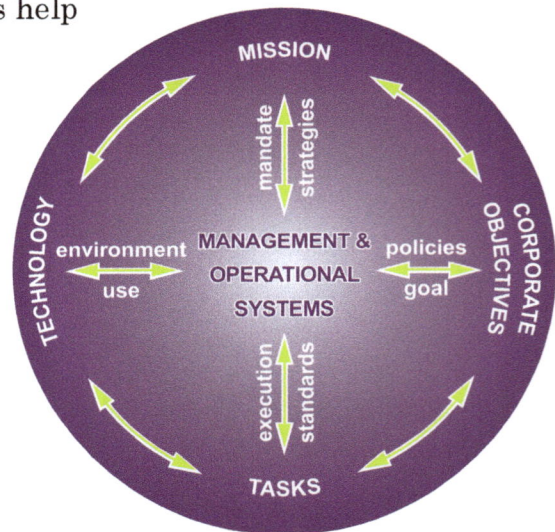

An organization is created by design. Its fundamental identity is defined by terms such as mission, strategy, and business objectives.

GENERAL REASONS
• mission
• philosophy
• strategy
• beliefs
• values
• business objective
• goal
• importance

To function, the organization must have money, equipment, materials, and people. To ensure activities are conducted in ways that support its mission, philosophy, strategies, and goals, management provides direction to employees by:
- identifying the work and tasks that must be carried out
- defining roles and responsibilities
- establishing management and administration to coordinate work
- developing policies, practices, procedures, and standards

All of the above items can be classified according to PEMEO. The reasons for the way the organization is designed are to prevent losses and optimize the use of resources, including people (LO-PEMEO).

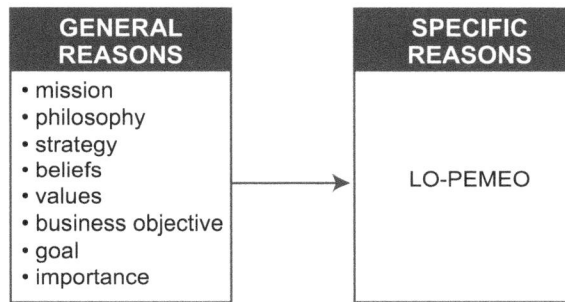

GENERAL REASONS	SPECIFIC REASONS
• mission • philosophy • strategy • beliefs • values • business objective • goal • importance	LO-PEMEO

When PEMEO comes together to be a productive unit, the effect is the creation of a work environment. Conditions, actions, and events associated with PEMEO define that work environment and the dynamics that are taking place.

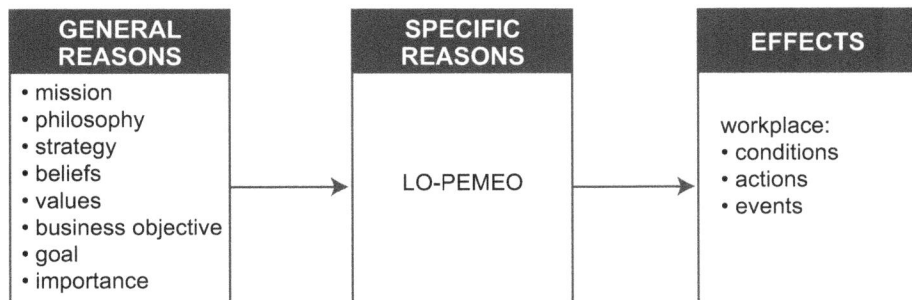

GENERAL REASONS	SPECIFIC REASONS	EFFECTS
• mission • philosophy • strategy • beliefs • values • business objective • goal • importance	LO-PEMEO	workplace: • conditions • actions • events

The results of production are a set of positive and negative consequences (LO). The types of consequence most important to an organization are those that affect PEMEO. For the organization, the most positive consequence is that production contributes to its mission and does so in a way that supports its beliefs and values. Unfortunately, negative consequences such as workplace injuries or equipment failure can also occur.

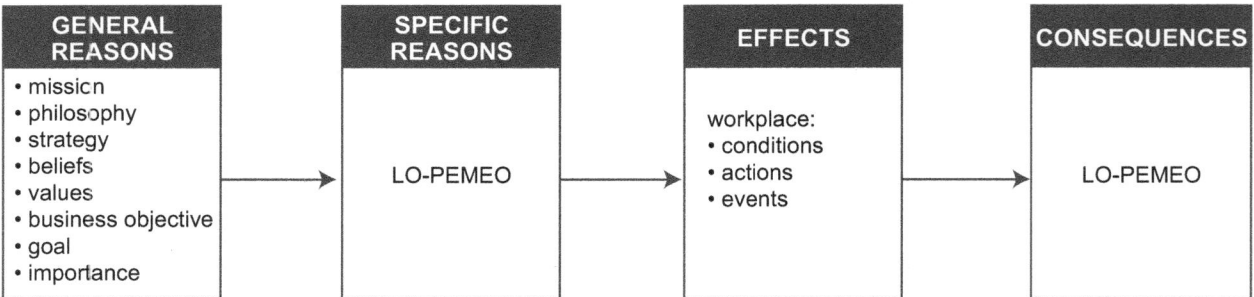

GENERAL REASONS	SPECIFIC REASONS	EFFECTS	CONSEQUENCES
• mission • philosophy • strategy • beliefs • values • business objective • goal • importance	LO-PEMEO	workplace: • conditions • actions • events	LO-PEMEO

Causes are often unintended and unpredictable (i.e., do not take place by design). For example:
- a natural gas line had a flaw
- the flaw *caused* the line to burst
- the escaping gas caused a fire (event)
- the fire *caused* the building to burn down (consequence)
- the employees are out of work (consequence)

Generally, one or more domains of PEMEO are the cause of the event and resulting consequences.

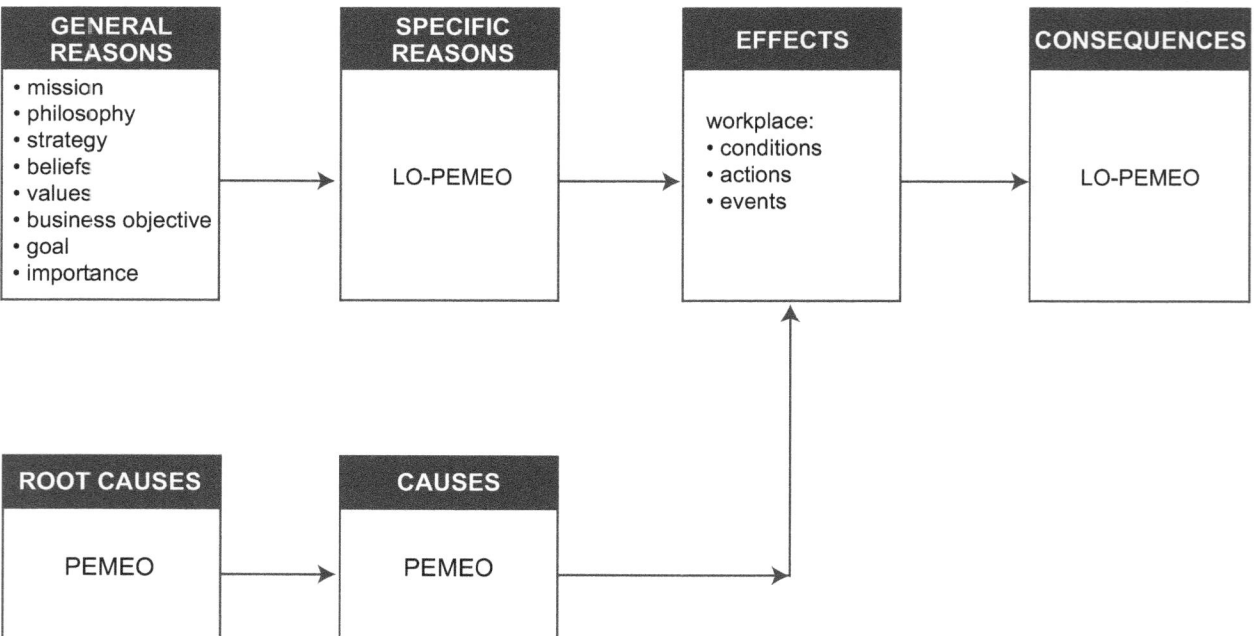

GENERAL REASONS	SPECIFIC REASONS	EFFECTS	CONSEQUENCES
• mission • philosophy • strategy • beliefs • values • business objective • goal • importance	LO-PEMEO	workplace: • conditions • actions • events	LO-PEMEO

ROOT CAUSES	CAUSES
PEMEO	PEMEO

As shown in the previous diagram, reasons, causes, effects, and consequences are closely related, PEMEO being the most common thread.

To determine the reasons or causes for a work environment being the way it is and for the way people work, you need to ask *Why?* questions about the conditions, actions, and events (the effects). When there are potentially negative consequences, you need to ask *Why?* questions to determine the causes, preferably before an incident occurs.

The following diagram shows the interrelationships between reasons, causes, effects, and consequences.

Interrelationship between Reasons, Causes, Effects, and Consequences

Start with an existing situation (effects), and ask Why? to identify the reasons and causes for the situation. If you know the consequences, you can determine the causes and reasons by first examining the conditions, actions, or events in the workplace (i.e., the effects that originated from the reasons and causes).

The type of *Why?* questions to ask and the answers to the questions relate to PEMEO because PEMEO is the most common thread within the organization and work environment. Start by examining the conditions, actions, and events in your work environment. Use the variables that are described in the previous section of this book. The variables give you direction for asking meaningful questions. The answers to the questions give meaning to *why* the variables are important to your organization, the job, and employees.

6.1 Reasons and Effects

Section 5 of this book described how you can use LO-PEMEO as a guide for identifying variables that are important to the job. In practice, you may often have to use the reverse strategy. You must determine *why* a certain variable is important. For example, determine:

- *why* a particular task is important
- *why* the steps to a task are performed in a specific order and way
- *why* specific safety precautions are taken
- *why* a particular event occurred
- *why* an internal customer requires a specific work assignment to be completed at a particular time
- *why* a variable for quality of a product is important
- *why* a piece of equipment must be operated at a specific setpoint or within a specific range

In industrial settings, the reasons often relate to the equipment itself or to the materials that are being manufactured, changed, or monitored. Equipment operation can be explained in terms of scientific concepts or principles and engineering design considerations. The explanation uses variables such as temperature, pressure, and force to describe how and why equipment works in a particular way, and why the variables (and their setpoints or operating ranges) are important for safe, effective, and efficient equipment operation and product quality.

Often equipment and material variables create a work condition that you must deal with. For example, an electric motor rotates because it is energized, creating a work condition. The rpm and power of the electric motor are determined by variables associated with equipment design and the quality of the electrical current being supplied to the motor at any given time.

Knowing why specific conditions exist can be important so that you can adjust your work effectively and make better decisions. For example, an operator must vary an auger's operation to meet production requirements. You must know the operating status of the auger to respond effectively to changes in throughput and stay clear of the auger when it is running. To carry out routine maintenance on the auger, the auger must not be operating and must be electrically locked out to prevent it from starting. The maintenance person must know the operating status of the auger before doing maintenance.

More detailed explanations of variables relating to materials and equipment are provided in the following books:
- *MatThink*
- *EquipThink*

You perform tasks for a reason. If you know the reasons for doing the work, you can be more effective in directing your efforts to achieve satisfactory results. For example, drywall being installed as a fire barrier will be covered with wood paneling. With this knowledge, you can pay less attention to marking the sheets and cutting them accurately and pay more attention to getting the work done quickly.

When performing tasks, some steps may be carried out in a particular way. If you know the reasons or importance for doing the steps in a particular way, you may be more conscientious when carrying out the steps. For example:
- When possible, shingles are applied on a roof starting from the bottom left corner for right-handed people and from the bottom right corner for left-handed people because the hand motions to place and nail the shingles are more natural and efficient.
- When energizing a large, high voltage breaker, electricians stand to the hinged side of the breaker panel and use their non-dominant hand to perform the action. Should the breaker explode, the hinged side of the door provides more protection than the opening side of the door. If an explosion

occurs, there is a possibility of the non-dominant hand being injured.

In the last example, note that the potential consequences provide the reasons for performing the task in a particular way. Consequences are described in more detail later in this section.

Events that occur in the workplace can be either planned or unplanned. If some workers are not informed of the planned event, from their perspective the effects are the same as if the event was not planned. From a safety perspective, unplanned events that have the potential of causing harm or do cause harm are called incidents.

Planned events are carried out for a reason, (e.g., a pump is taken out of service for repair). Operators must know that the pump will be out of service so that they can adjust their work. Knowing how long the pump will be out of service may affect how they respond. Knowing why the pump needs service could affect how operators do their work in the future. Operators may be able to adjust how they operate the pump to extend pump life.

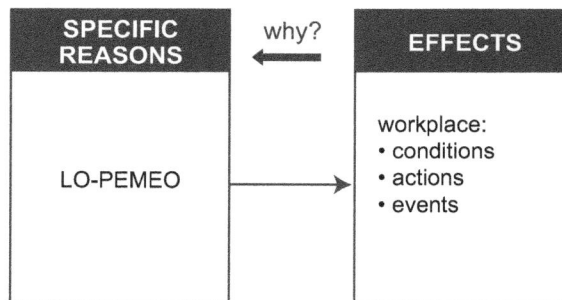

Specific Reasons (LO-PEMEO) for the Effects (Conditions, Actions, Events)

Often you can determine the immediate reason for an effect by examining one or more domains of PEMEO (i.e., the answers to asking why about the effect involve PEMEO). A more general reason can often be identified by asking the *reason for the reason* or the *why for the why*. For example, the suction pressure to a compressor is set at the maximum recommended limit. The reason for the high suction pressure is to maximize throughput. The reason the throughput is maximized may be to maximize revenue or meet customer orders. Often the reason for the reason will be an organization's mission, philosophy, belief, value, strategy, or business goal.

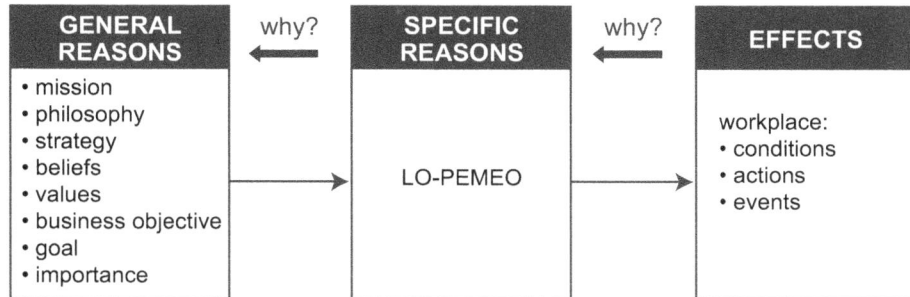

GENERAL REASONS	why?	SPECIFIC REASONS	why?	EFFECTS
• mission • philosophy • strategy • beliefs • values • business objective • goal • importance		LO-PEMEO		workplace: • conditions • actions • events

Effect (variables), Specific Reasons (LO-PEMEO), and General Reasons (beliefs, etc.)

Sometimes organizations have policies that can make your work more difficult. If you understand the reasons for the policies, you may be more willing to tolerate or support the policies.

LEARNING ACTIVITY 7

Reasons

If you know the reasons for doing the work and why the work processes and conditions are the way they are, you can be more effective in directing your efforts to achieve satisfactory results.

1. To determine why an equipment variable is important, you must _____.

    a. define the function of the equipment

    b. identify the scientific concepts and principles involved

    c. determine how the equipment design applies scientific concepts to achieving the desired results

    d. all of the above

2. Often, technical training resources give reasons why the technology, tasks, steps, and conditions are important. Why does the training provide reasons?

   a. If you know the reasons or importance for doing the steps of a task in a particular way, you will be more conscientious in carrying out the steps.

   b. If you know the reasons for doing the work, you can be more effective at achieving the desired results.

   c. If you know why specific conditions exist, you can adjust your work effectively and make better decisions.

   d. all of the above

   e. a and b only

3. You are using a countertop blender in your kitchen.

   a. How does the blender blend food?

   _____

   _____

   b. What are the technical reasons for starting the blender slowly and then gradually increasing the speed?

   _____

   _____

4. Identify a policy in your organization that makes your work more difficult.

   _____

   _____

   a. Give reasons why your organization adopted the policy.

   _____

   _____

   _____

b. To what degree do you believe the policy addresses the concerns? Explain your position.

☐ less than adequate

☐ about right

☐ overkill

_____

_____

_____

6.2 Effects and Consequences

In addition to determining reasons for a specific variable (condition, action, or event), examine the consequences of the variable. Some considerations relative to consequences include:

- Of all possible consequences, those affecting PEMEO are the most important to organizations.
- A condition, employee action, or event impacting one PEMEO domain most likely impacts other PEMEO domains.
- If a job variable changes, consequences can also change.
- You must know the consequences for PEMEO if a variable changes or does not change when it is supposed to.
- Over time, variables can slowly change, requiring you to compensate by making incremental changes to the way you perform the work.
- You may be required to document the effect, consequences, reasons, and response to an event.

NOTE   Common language addresses these thinking strategies in the following order: reasons, causes, consequences. However, in this book, it is more logical to explain the thinking strategies in the following order: reasons, effect, consequences, cause.

The purpose for operating equipment and for employees to do work is to achieve specific results or outcomes. However, the actual results or outcomes may be different than expected. Often, work can be done in different ways to achieve the same results. There may be advantages and disadvantages for using different methods to do the work. Conditions such as seasonal temperatures or material quality can affect the results. The consequences of an event can be positive or negative, depending on the circumstances. Results, outcomes, and the significance of the results or outcomes are all consequences of specific conditions, actions, or events.

You must be able to *predict* consequences and take the appropriate action to achieve desired results and minimize loss. Predicting consequences can be difficult because a change in conditions, actions, or events can produce a different set of consequences. You must continually look for consequences that have a significant impact on the corporation, the job, and employees. In some cases, you must identify loss control measures to reduce the risk of experiencing losses.

There are many possible consequences for a given situation, depending on whom or what the consequences affect. For businesses, the most important consequences are those that impact on PEMEO, especially the corporate goals.

NOTE

Asking questions about the impact on PEMEO is usually sufficient for identifying consequences that are relevant. However, be conscious of your own expertise, interests, and beliefs that can bias the types of question you ask. The prerequisite books listed in the introduction address the domains of PEMEO. Each book emphasizes *asking the right questions* as a strategy to identify what is important to employee, job, and corporate performance.

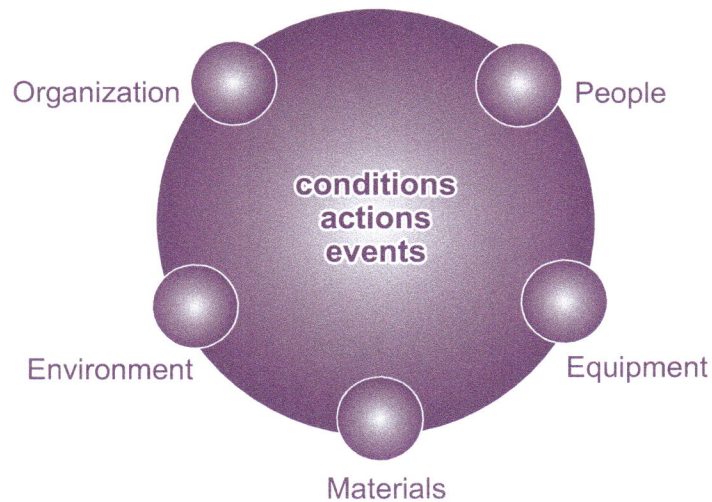

Conditions, Actions, and Events Impact on PEMEO

A variable (condition, action, or event) that impacts one PEMEO domain often impacts other PEMEO domains. For example, a hazardous substance could cause harm to people. That substance might also be corrosive and cause damage to equipment, materials, and the environment. The business may experience costs to reduce the potential of losses and, should an incident occur, lose public support.

When you understand the consequences for a given variable (condition, action, or event), you can find ways to optimize the use of assets and reduce the risk of losses.

Reasons can explain static conditions and normal work practices which lead to desirable consequences, especially optimization of assets and the minimization of losses. However, if a job variable changes, consequences can also change. Or, if a job variable does not change when it is supposed to, the desired result (consequence) may not be achieved.

For you to be effective in performing tasks and making decisions, you must predict the potential consequences should variables change or something goes wrong. Identifying *what can go wrong* can be very difficult because the question is too broad—it can be very difficult to know what questions to ask. To help you focus your thinking, consider what can go wrong with PEMEO. Ask *What if... ?* questions about conditions, actions, and events that could occur and cause PEMEO to function poorly, behave abnormally, or fail. If there is a concern, determine the immediate effect. If there is a potential for loss, take action to reduce the potential of an incident occurring and/or the severity of the consequences.

NOTE

SafeThink uses a structured critical thinking strategy to ask *What if ... ?* questions to identify the immediate effect and potential consequences that affect people's safety. In this book, *What if... ?* questions are asked to determine the immediate effect and potential consequences for all domains of PEMEO.

The following table provides some examples of asking *What if... ?* questions to determine the consequences.

What can go wrong with PEMEO		
Domain	**What if . . . ?** (*conditions, actions, events*)	**Immediate Effect**
People	What if I put the crates in the alleyway?	Workers on the other side would have their escape route blocked.
	What if I don't close the valve fully?	Toxic gas will leak to the atmosphere.
	What if I suffer fatigue because I have worked long hours to complete a job?	My ability to think through the work and concentrate is diminished.
Equipment	What if the conveyor starts?	My arm would be caught in the drive chain.
	What if the clamp on the winch line breaks?	The load will fall to the ground and the cable will snake through the air.
	What if the equipment is put on computer control?	The equipment will start and stop without warning.
Materials	What if high-grade sockets are replaced with low-grade sockets?	The sockets could break when the usual force is applied.
	What if the materials can easily disintegrate?	Dust will contaminate the atmosphere.
	What if the wood pry lever breaks?	I will fall backwards.
		The wood will split into two long sharp points.
Environment	What if mice invade the storage area?	Shelves and supplies will be covered with infectious droppings.
	What if the number of workers on site increases 4-fold?	The variety and dynamics of work would increase dramatically.
	What if I step out of the vehicle onto icy pavement?	I could slip.
Organization	What if the renovators are painting?	The vapors will get into the ventilation system and travel to other parts of the building.
	What if the supplier replaces neoprene gloves with rubber gloves?	The solvent will rapidly penetrate the gloves and contact skin.
	What if the crew is short staffed?	Completing the job on time will be difficult.

You may have difficulties in asking quality *What if. . .?* questions that apply to the Organization domain. Here are some examples of conditions, actions, and events related to the Organization domain that can affect PEMEO. Check off the examples that most likely apply to your job and work group.

☐ poor scheduling (timing of activities)

☐ not following coordination plans

☐ a change in the work process

☐ shortage of staff

☐ lack of competent workers assigned to a specific task

☐ policy that can cause harm under certain conditions (e.g., wearing PPE in extremely hot environments can lead to heat stroke if rest periods are not taken frequently)

☐ work group introduces new hazard

☐ third party fails to maintain equipment/facilities

☐ supplier changes standards or composition of components or materials

☐ unpredicted large customer order

☐ cancellation or delay of large customer order (e.g., may have excessive inventory on site)

☐ failure to communicate priorities

☐ lack of documentation

☐ roles and responsibilities for work assignment not clear

☐ administrative process inadequate for maintaining inventory

☐ failure to carry out routine safety inspections

☐ failure to follow up/correct identified safety deficiencies

The previous table listed some immediate effects of conditions, actions, or events associated with PEMEO. The immediate effect may not be a direct consequence for PEMEO. However, the consequence of the immediate effect may affect one or more domains of PEMEO. For example, if a surface is slippery and the effect is that someone falls, the fall itself does not affect the person—however, your reaction and the impact due to the fall can have a variety of consequences, depending on the conditions:

- the surface may be flat
- the surface may be cluttered with sharp, jagged objects
- the fall may be into a vat or lagoon
- the fall may be into moving equipment components
- the fall could be in the path of moving equipment
- the person falling could be carrying materials or equipment that can get damaged
- if another person is nearby, that person could get hit by the one who is falling or by the objects he or she is carrying
- the person falling can react in an attempt to recover from the fall and strain back muscles
- the person falling may not get hurt at all

When asking *What if... ?* questions, first determine the immediate effect. The immediate effect may or may not be a consequence for PEMEO. Then ask yourself if the immediate effect can have or lead to consequences for PEMEO.

What if... ? questions are about conditions, actions, and events and, most often, about changes in conditions, actions, and events. Changes can often be defined in terms of variables.

For variables that can affect you, other people, the job, or your organization, ask yourself what is normal or ideal, and then determine how a change in variables can have negative consequences for PEMEO. For example, regarding equipment, ask, *If... (the variables are not within specifications or do not behave as expected)... what are the consequences for PEMEO?* If the consequences are significant, determine how you should respond to the situation. You may determine the response partly by determining the reasons or causes for the variable to change or not change and partly by determining the lines and limits of authority for your job position. For example, at the beginning of your shift, you notice that a furnace damper, normally set at 60% open, is now fully open. A fully open damper can cause excessive heating of the exhaust stack (consequence). The employee on the previous shift must have been aware of the damper position because of an alarm being triggered. To determine if you must respond to the situation, you must determine the reason or cause for the fully open damper. Then, if there is a need to respond, you must determine which response is appropriate for your particular job position.

One variable will often affect other variables. If a variable changes, you may have to make adjustments to equipment, materials, and work processes to get the optimal results. Unfortunately, there is often a trade-off in achieving the desired results. For example:

- It is aesthetically desirable for some customers to have a smooth driveway leading to a garage. However, a smooth driveway covered with snow, ice, or water is slippery, increasing the risk of someone falling and, if the driveway is sloped, difficulty in driving. For any given customer, what degree of smoothness is desired? What are the processes and costs to adjust the smoothness? What are the consequences to PEMEO if the surface is too smooth or too rough for a given customer?

- An operator opens a flow control valve further to increase the flow to a particular process so that the process meets downstream throughput commitments. What impact does the increased flow have on the upstream process? Is the upstream process supplying more than one process and, if so, will the increase in throughput to one process starve the other process? What are the consequences for PEMEO when the product flow is increased to the particular process?

- Maintenance personnel must install a refurbished head on a large natural gas engine. The installation process must be such that the head will not experience uneven stress when in use and the gasket between the head and block does not develop a leak (critical variables). The manufacturer recommends torquing the head bolts down following a specific pattern and to a specific amount.

What if the bolts are unevenly torqued, torqued too much, or not torqued enough—what are the consequences for PEMEO?

In the last example, the actions of the maintenance person could have significant impacts on PEMEO. Operating and maintenance best practices can contribute to improving equipment function, reliability, and life. Some practices can create downgrading incidents. Sudden and dramatic operating moves such as rapidly opening a valve or jerking on a winch line can cause excessive forces on equipment, reducing equipment life or causing component failure. Always consider the consequences of your actions for PEMEO.

Using a rigorous approach to identify which variables have a significant impact on PEMEO can seem very time consuming. However, it usually becomes apparent which variables can be disregarded and which variables require special attention. For example, an X-ray technician starts an X-ray machine by carrying out the following major steps:

1. *perform pre-start adjustments of machine settings*
2. *switch on the power*
3. *after the machine has warmed up for five minutes, make final adjustments to machine settings*

Step one can probably be completed without significant problems or consequences because the equipment does not respond to most of the adjustments (the X-ray machine is turned off). There is probably limited risk of harm to the operator or equipment. Is there an efficient way of completing step one?

Step two is more critical because the machine must respond to operator action and there is a possibility that the machine may not power up. **What if** the X-ray machine does not start when the power is turned on?

Step three may have one or more significant consequences because the X-ray machine must respond to the operator's actions. Are there any final adjustments that the operator must pay special attention to? **What if** the machine doesn't respond as expected? Can the operator be exposed to X-rays? If yes, could other PEMEO domains be affected? Is there an efficient way of completing step three?

When you carry out a step of a task, you need a means for measuring results. Standards define how well or to what degree of excellence the work has to be done and provide a means of assessing performance. Standards can apply to the results of performance for the task as a whole and to each step of the task. Standards can often be expressed in terms of quality, quantity, time, and timeliness. The standards for the tasks you do originate from within your organization and from outside sources such as government regulations and standards associations.

In the workplace, standards often relate to:
• creating change
• confirming and monitoring actions, status of variables, and conditions
• communicating and documenting actions, status of variables, and conditions

When you perform a step of a task, ask yourself:
• How do I know I have performed this step satisfactorily?
• What can go wrong?
• What do I do to minimize loss if I perform the step poorly?

The book *WorkThink* provides a more complete explanation of standards, including examples.

When asking yourself questions, use elimination to make the thinking process efficient. Start by asking yourself general questions such as *Can I or others be harmed?* (i.e., loss to people). If you think there is a possibility of harm, then ask the six *SafeThink* questions:
• Does the work involve hazardous materials?
• Does the work involve objects, motion, or force that could cause harm?
• Does the work involve non-ambient conditions that could cause harm?
• Is current or static electricity a factor in doing the work?

- Is radiation present when doing the work?
- Could changes lead to or create a hazardous situation?

If you say no to the first question, move to the next question. If you say yes, then you ask yourself the critical question: *Are there any conditions, actions, or events that can lead to or create a hazardous situation?*

If you say *no* then you move onto the next question in the list of six questions. However, if you say *Yes, there are conditions, actions, or events that can lead to or create a hazardous situation*, you ask questions about consequences and controls.

The *SafeThink* book provides comprehensive instruction on using a structured critical thinking strategy to identify and predict hazardous situations.

Sometimes, understanding how the technology works (reasons) can make it easier to identify significant consequences if a variable does not respond to your actions as expected. For example, you are lighting the burner on a piece of equipment by opening the fuel line to the burner and introducing a source of ignition. **What if** the burner does not light immediately? The fuel gas rapidly accumulates in the burning chamber. If you continue to try to light the burner, the excessive fuel gas could suddenly ignite, causing flames to discharge through the ignition port and air intake, burning you. For what length of time can you continue to try lighting the burner before you are at risk of being burnt? If the burner doesn't light within the time limit, what should you do?

NOTE

Asking *What if... ?* questions is an effective strategy for predicting consequences that can put your customer's business and people at risk. Preventative measures can then be taken to reduce the probability of the incident and potential severity of the consequences.

Over a long period of time, equipment condition and function can change because of wear, corrosion, and fouling. In some cases, the consequences can be very serious, as in the case of a pipe or vessel becoming weak due to corrosion and then rupturing. Operator and maintenance activities may have to be modified to accommodate slow changes in work conditions. For example, operators may have to make incremental changes to the flow rate of products going to a heat exchanger as the tubes in the exchanger slowly accumulate a buildup of scale. A scale buildup reduces the efficiency of heat being exchanged. Maintenance staff may have to do reactive maintenance more often and more extensively as equipment wears and becomes dysfunctional. For some tasks, your organization may have documented the adjustments required to counter changes in equipment conditions. Your organization may also have a documented emergency response plan when consequences for PEMEO could be immediate and severe.

You may have to respond immediately to abnormal emergency conditions or events to minimize the severity of the consequences. To respond effectively, you must understand your role and responsibilities and the potential consequences for PEMEO. Your organization may have an emergency response plan in which you are required to carry out specific actions. Make sure you understand the response plan. When working, ask *What if... ?* questions to determine what can go wrong and the possible immediate effects. Then ask yourself these questions:
- Could I or others become ill and/or injured?
- Could property, equipment, or materials be damaged?
- What should be my first response if an incident occurs?
- What can I do to minimize the possibility of an incident occurring and/or the potential severity of the consequences?

For many of the incidents identified by the *What if... ?* questions, you will be more effective in your response by:
- determining in advance the response you would make
- rehearsing your response in your mind by imagining responding to the incident. Rehearsing increases the possibility that you will respond immediately and effectively.

Ask yourself the following questions about variables:
- *Which variables are important to the job?*
- *Why are the variables important? (reason)*

- *What are the desirable specifications for the variables?*
- *Which variables can be controlled?*
- *Which variables can change?*
- *Why does a variable change? (reason or cause)*
- *What are the indicators that a variable has changed?*
- *What happens when a variable changes? (consequence for PEMEO)*
- *What must be done in response to a change in a variable? (reasons, limits of authority)*
- *How do work processes (operations and maintenance) affect the variables? (consequences for PEMEO)*
- *What are my roles and responsibilities if the consequences for PEMEO are immediate and severe? (i.e., my response to an abnormal or emergency situation)*

After answering these questions, you will have a more complete knowledge about variables affecting your job. With increased knowledge, you reduce the number of questions you need to continually ask yourself about your work and work environment.

Corporate goals can also be treated as variables. Within a department, corporate goals address issues such as safety, business image, reliability, and cost control. These goals may be ordered in priority—safety and environment are often on top of the list. However, specific corporate goals and their priorities may vary from department to department. In some cases, departments may be in conflict if goal priorities are different. For example, the safety and loss control department wants to do site audits within a specific time frame. The sites have productivity schedules that must be met and audits disrupt production.

Knowing the corporate goals and the priority of goals for your department and other departments is important for understanding how your work affects other departments and vice-versa. You may then be able to adjust or coordinate your work to reduce the negative impact on other departments. Being aware of other department priorities may also be useful in planning your work to reduce the impact they have on your work.

Consequences

This learning activity will help you to refine your thinking skills to *predict* consequences and take the appropriate action to achieve desired results and minimize loss.

1. A condition, employee action, or event impacting on one PEMEO domain often impacts other PEMEO domains.

   a. true

   b. false

2. When you understand the consequences of a particular effect (condition, action, or event), you can be proactive in finding ways to optimize the use of assets and reduce the risk of losses.

   a. true

   b. false

3. If a variable changes, you may have to make adjustments to equipment, materials, and work processes to get optimal results.

   a. true

   b. false

4. To make an effective response to an abnormal or emergency condition, you must consider _____.

   a. the consequences of the situation

   b. your roles and responsibilities in responding to the situation

   c. your supervisor's expectations

   d. what is important to the organization

   e. the priority of corporate goals

   f. all of the above

5. You are using a countertop blender in your kitchen.

   a. What are the consequences of using the blender according to the manufacturer's instructions?

_____

_____

b. What are the potential consequences for PEMEO of failing to fit the lid on tightly before starting the blender?

_____

_____

_____

c. What are the potential consequences for PEMEO of using a spoon to push the food into the blender during operation?

_____

_____

_____

d. What are the potential consequences for PEMEO of cleaning the blender without unplugging it from the electrical source?

_____

_____

_____

e. What are the potential consequences for PEMEO of not cleaning the blender thoroughly before re-assembling the parts and using the blender again?

_____

_____

_____

_____

NOTE

Questions 5a to 5e were generated by asking *What if... ?* questions to predict consequences that affect PEMEO. If an incident were to occur, the undesired action would become the cause for the consequences.

6.3 Causes, Effects, and Consequences

In business, reasons provide the motive and the explanation for effects (conditions, actions, and events) that achieve specific desirable results and minimize risk (positive consequences). However, some effects (conditions, actions, or events) are unplanned and can often have a negative impact on PEMEO. Causes provide the explanation about why unplanned conditions, actions, or events occur. Often causes are not initially known and an investigation (troubleshooting) may be required and corrective action determined. The following illustration shows that many causes originate because of PEMEO. The causes create an effect that can have serious consequences for PEMEO.

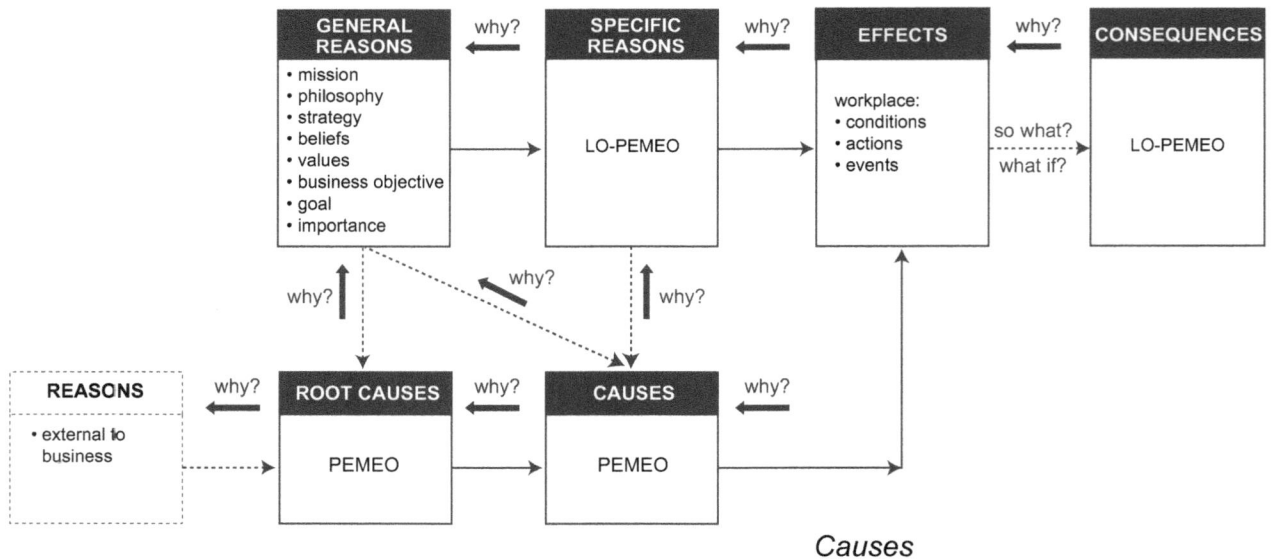

Causes

If the effect can cause serious losses to PEMEO, an immediate operator, maintenance, or emergency response may be required to minimize the negative consequences. For long-term prevention, businesses can respond to an undesirable effect by treating the symptom, the immediate cause, or the root cause (the cause for the cause or reason for the cause).

The following table shows the relationships between effect, causes, and root causes or reasons.

	Observation	Action
Effect (symptom)	an engine has excessive emissions (CO, NO+)	put in a catalytic converter to convert emissions to acceptable products
Immediate Cause	worn piston rings	replace the worn piston rings to reduce the production of emissions
Root Cause (or Reason)	wrong type of engine oil is used	use the correct type of engine oil to reduce the rate of piston ring wear

In the engine example shown in the previous table, if the root cause is not determined, the engine will continue to experience premature piston ring wear after being repaired. The consequences for PEMEO include unnecessary maintenance costs and equipment downtime, excessive emissions, increased fuel and oil consumption, and reduced engine power. Work performed by operators and maintenance staff is also affected.

NOTE

The reasons for the root cause can originate from within the business or from outside the business. In the example of using the wrong engine oil, the reason for using the wrong oil could be that the company was trying to save money, employees don't know the importance of using a specific type of oil, or the manufacturer did not understand the conditions in which the engine operates and therefore did not recommend a suitable oil product.

When problems occur in the workplace, the cause(s) for the problems may not be immediately known. In these cases, you may have to troubleshoot. The headings in the following table outline the steps of a basic troubleshooting strategy that you may find helpful. A simplified example is provided.

Condition	Possible Causes	Diagnosis	Response	Indicators of Correction
Engine missing (runs roughly)	– bad fuel – spark plugs worn – ignition wire damaged	engine analyzer shows poor electrical ignition	change spark plugs	engine runs smoothly

Condition: clearly define the abnormal condition, symptom, or effect.

Possible Causes: based on the symptoms, identify the possible causes. You may need to:
• consider similar incidents
• review the histories of the equipment. Some companies have extensive databases on equipment histories.
• use troubleshooting charts
• determine when the problem started and the conditions, actions, and events that existed at that time
• Ask *What if... ?* questions to relate effect to cause. For equipment, materials, and work processes, it is helpful to understand the principles, concepts, components, and materials properties and characteristics relating to the problem.

Diagnosis: if the cause cannot be easily identified, a formal diagnostic process (e.g., using diagnostic equipment and software) may be carried out. Sometimes a formal failure analysis process may be carried out to determine root causes.

Response: the impact of the problem on PEMEO and the available responses are two key determining factors in selecting a response. Other than an emergency response (described in the previous section) possible immediate responses include:
• shutting down equipment and processes until a reliable fix is initiated

- stopping work until the problem is fixed
- making a temporary fix
- bringing in temporary resources such as portable equipment and additional staff
- using other available equipment and materials
- doing nothing

Using the corporate goals and considering the priority of the goals can help in selecting the best immediate course of action.

Longer-term responses may involve addressing the immediate cause or root cause of the problem.

Indicators of Correction: after the problem is fixed you need to determine if the fix is satisfactory and reliable. To determine the effectiveness of the fix, you need to identify criteria for judging whether or not the corrections have resolved the problem satisfactorily. For example, the equipment functions as designed, the materials meet the desired specifications, the rate of production is as expected, and the product or service meets customer expectations. For long-term solutions, you may also want to identify ways to reduce the probability of the problem recurring or the severity of consequences should the problem occur again.

For complex problems, a multi-discipline team of specialists such as operators, maintenance staff, engineers, and vendors may be used. The team determines the root cause of the problem, identifies possible corrective courses of action, and selects the best solution. These activities require the team to determine reasons, causes, and consequences for the specific conditions, actions, and events (effect).

Determining causes and making an effective *decision* in the best interest of your organization requires you to keep the *big picture* in mind, that is, the business context. The following illustration shows the relationship between tasks, management and operational systems, technology, corporate objectives or goals, and mission (constituents). All five constituents are integral to making an effective decision in the best interest of your organization. The book *JobThink* addresses the constituents and their relationships to each other at the job level to help you determine how to direct your efforts effectively to contribute to job and corporate performance.

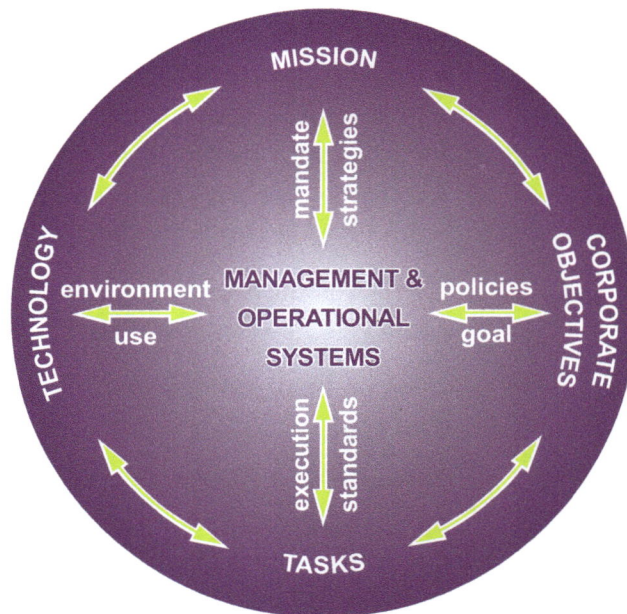

Relationship between constituents

Using reasons, causes, effects, and consequences is an important strategy for you to do your job well—minimize the risk of losses, optimize the use of assets, and make effective decisions. You must be able to think through the reasons, causes, and consequences for specific effects (conditions, actions, and events). Ideally you should apply the thinking strategy before, during, and after completing work assignments. Industrial businesses use the strategy formally when carrying out loss control and risk management activities. Two loss control activities relating to tasks are:

- identifying tasks that have the potential of creating severe losses to PEMEO (critical tasks)
- conducting a hazard analysis of these critical tasks and building in controls to reduce the risk of experiencing losses

Many risk management analyses focus on losses with only minimal consideration given to identifying ways to optimize assets. A more comprehensive method for analyzing tasks is to apply the LO-PEMEO strategy. Several thinking strategies are fundamental to applying the LO-PEMEO strategy:

- identifying work variables, conditions, actions, and events
- determining the reasons and causes for variables to change
- determining the consequences for PEMEO

LEARNING ACTIVITY 9

Causes, effects, and consequences

This learning activity will help you refine your thinking skills to identify causes for a problem, the potential consequences, and criteria for selecting solutions that fit within your organization's context.

1. Why is it important to discover the root cause for negative consequences?

    _____

    _____

2. Other than responding to an emergency, what are the two most important factors to consider when deciding on a response to a work problem?

    _____

    _____

3. Why is it important to have criteria for judging whether a problem is fixed satisfactorily or not?

    _____

    _____

4. In your workplace, identify a production problem that has occurred or could occur.

    a. What would be your first response to the problem?

        _____

        _____

    b. What are the steps you would take to determine the cause of the problem?

        _____

        _____

        _____

c. What do you think is most likely required to temporarily fix the problem?

_____

_____

_____

_____

d. What would be long-term solutions to reduce the probability of the problem occurring again and/or reduce the severity of consequences to PEMEO?

_____

_____

_____

Conduct a Loss/ Optimization Analysis Using LO-PEMEO

The LO-PEMEO thinking strategy is a powerful tool for identifying what is important to corporate, job, and employee performance. The strategy focuses on work conditions, actions, and events to identify consequences for PEMEO and ways to improve efficiencies and reduce the risk of losses.

There are advantages to using the LO-PEMEO thinking strategy when analyzing a task. One advantage is that using a rigorous process demonstrates both corporate and legislative due diligence. The list of questions for each domain identifies the most important questions you can ask to optimize your performance and prevent downgrading the work or production.

There are one or two *Exemplary Worker* books for each LO-PEMEO domain (see page 2 for a list of books). Each book lists the most critical questions you can ask yourself. Combining the list of questions from each book provides a comprehensive list of questions for conducting a loss/ optimization analysis of a task (critical task analysis).

Often a critical task analysis is carried out by a group of specialists such as operators, maintenance personnel, safety specialists, environmental specialists, and engineers. Each specialist has expertise and knowledge about government regulations, safety precautions, and methods of work that are important to doing a comprehensive analysis.

For any given task and work environment, the list of questions important to the person doing the work is much smaller (by elimination). For each LO-PEMEO domain, the most important questions depend on the type of work you do. Using *Environment* as an example:

If you are a maintenance person:
- *Is this waste harmful to the environment?*
- *If yes: how do I store or dispose of it?*

If you are a process operator:
- *Will a pollutant be discharged to the environment?*
- *If yes: Could the amount or rate of discharge exceed government regulations?*
- *If yes: How do I know the amount or rate is excessive?*
- *If an excessive amount or rate of pollutant is being discharged, what do I do about it?*

Recap of key points: Using a limited number of LO-PEMEO questions that apply to your job and workplace is a powerful thinking strategy for optimizing your performance and that of the job. You are also preventing downgrading incidents. Of course, you need to actually answer the questions. If you know your work and the technology well, you probably have the answers; if you don't have an answer, ask others. The point being made is: Ask yourself LO-PEMEO questions. By asking yourself questions (and seeking the answers), you are more vigilant and thorough in thinking through your work.

Example of applying the LO-PEMEO strategy: The following table illustrates an application of the LO-PEMEO strategy to a single action. The questions apply to making a change to a piece of equipment in a process or manufacturing line. Although the example identifies a specific piece of equipment, the questions that are asked could apply to making a *change* to any type of equipment in a production line.

Action: Turn the feed auger control knob to 480 rpm to increase the auger speed.

LO–PEMEO: Loss, Optimization–People, Equipment, Materials, Environment, Organization

Questions: You ask yourself and seek answers to each question. If the answer is no or you think the question is irrelevant for this situation, move to the next question.

Questions You Ask Yourself
Loss-People • *Does the action affect the operator's safety? No.* • *Does the action affect others up or downstream of auger? Possibly. In what ways? What hazards?*
Optimization-People • *Is there a special way of carrying out the action? Possibly. The auger speed may have to be increased rapidly or slowly.*
Loss and Optimization of Equipment • *Does increasing the auger speed cause additional wear/stress on the auger? Possibly.* • *Does the increased throughput cause stress on upstream or downstream equipment? Possibly.* • *Is there an optimal auger running speed that minimizes wear and possible failure? Possibly.* • *Is there an optimal auger running speed that makes the most efficient use of energy? Possibly.*
Loss and Optimization of Materials • *Can this auger speed damage the raw materials? Possibly.* • *Will some product be wasted or spilled at this auger speed?* • *What is the ideal auger speed to optimize both upstream and downstream processes?* • *What is the ideal auger speed that causes the least damage to the materials?*

(continued)

Questions You Ask Yourself
Loss and Optimization of the Environment
• *Does this auger speed cause some product to enter the environment?*
• *Can the product cause harm to the environment?*
Loss and Optimization of Organization
• *Do other operators need to be informed that the auger speed is going to be changed?*
• *Does the operator have to document the changed auger speed?*
• *What is the optimal auger speed to maximize productivity and maintain product quality?*
Note: *some LO-PEMEO domains have been combined because loss and optimization issues are closely related. Generally, when you optimize a domain you reduce losses and vice versa.*

Using LO-PEMEO to Identify Relevant Questions

The preceding table identifies basic questions about:
• the consequences that the action of changing the auger speed has on PEMEO
• ways of improving the efficiency and effectiveness of PEMEO

Having determined the consequences for PEMEO of increasing the auger speed to 480 rpm, you could ask yourself if the increase in rpm is reasonable considering the potential for losses.

You could explore further by asking additional questions:
• *What is the reason for adjusting the auger speed to 480 rpm?*
• *Is it possible that the auger will not speed up to the desired rpm?*
• *What is your response (within lines and limits of authority) if the auger doesn't speed up?*
• *What caused the auger to fail to respond to your adjustments?*

To increase your knowledge about the auger's operation, you could ask additional questions relating to changes in auger rpm:
• *Is there a maximum and minimum rpm limit for operating the auger?*

- *What are the reasons for the rpm limits? Is it equipment design, material damage, limits to the throughput of upstream and downstream processes?*
- *What are the consequences for PEMEO if the rpm limits are exceeded?*
- *What are the indicators the auger's rpm is approaching or exceeding the rpm limits?*
- *What is my response if the auger rpm approaches or exceeds the rpm limits?*
- *What are the causes for the auger rpm to change without operator input (e.g., changes in the physical characteristics and mass of the materials, a lack of materials flowing to the auger)?*

To prepare yourself to respond effectively to abnormal operation or failure, you could also ask general questions regarding what could go wrong (e.g., the input or the discharge end of the auger plugs up):

- *How do I know there is a problem?*
- *What is the impact on PEMEO?*
- *What is the cause of the problem?*
- *What do I do about it, if anything?*

NOTE These questions address change, effect and its indicators, cause, consequence, and operator response within lines and limits of authority.

All possible LO-PEMEO combinations result in ten categories (L-P, O-P, etc.) that could apply to any work situation. Initially, applying all ten categories to every work situation seems overwhelming. To use the LO-PEMEO strategy efficiently and effectively, several considerations must be taken into account:

- To be expedient, you could use the process of elimination. For a given situation, determine if a LO-PEMEO domain or category may be relevant and then concentrate on only the relevant domains or categories. If you are very familiar with the specific work conditions, actions, or events that impact on PEMEO, you can often recognize optimization opportunities and loss issues.

- To determine if a LO-PEMEO category is relevant, you must recognize specific factors (conditions, actions, events) that are associated with each category. For example, there are only six general types of hazard (e.g., hazardous materials, electricity) that could cause harm to people. For equipment, a sudden and dramatic change in a variable can often cause damage or shorten equipment life. When you recognize that a condition, action, or event could affect a LO-PEMEO category, you should investigate further. Determine if there is, in fact, potential for loss or opportunities for optimization and, if so, the controls to reduce the risk of loss and improve efficiency and effectiveness. This strategy requires you to be able to recognize (or memorize) the factors affecting each domain. You can then do a mental search to determine if each factor is applicable. Each LO-PEMEO book lists the most critical questions you can ask yourself.
- If a factor affects one PEMEO domain, you should investigate to determine if other domains are also affected.
- As a general strategy to identify issues relevant to your work and job, always question yourself about the implications of the task and workplace (cause, consequences, reasons, what if: it doesn't work, it behaves differently, or a variable is changed). Ask yourself questions about ways to reduce losses and improve the efficiency and effectiveness of PEMEO. Having asked yourself these types of question, you can eliminate most of the questions as not being important for the specific context, and then concentrate on answering the questions that are applicable to the situation.
- Having asked questions about how things work and how to work them, you have gained critical knowledge and do not have to ask those types of questions again. You can concentrate on assessing the conditions of your work environment and on changes created by doing work and by events. You goals are to determine ways to efficiently achieve the desired results and predict consequences for PEMEO.

When you identify optimization and loss control issues, you need to identify ways to improve performance and reduce the risk of losses. The following table provides examples of performance improvement strategies and loss control measures that can be taken when carrying out work.

Using LO-PEMEO to assess work is a rigorous method for identifying issues important to your performance and that of the job and the organization. Continually asking yourself questions helps you to remain vigilant while working and to perform exemplary work.

Performance Improvement Strategies and Loss Control Measures	Examples
Gather all the items needed to do the work before starting the task.	• Think through the steps of the task and itemize the equipment, parts, and safety items you will need. • At the beginning of some procedures, the equipment, parts, and safety items will be listed.
Ensure the worksite is safe before doing the work.	• Visually inspect the work area to ensure there are no hazardous situations, including those created when working with others. • Conduct a pre-job hazard assessment with others who will be working with you or in your vicinity. • Confirm that control measures are effective (e.g., confirm that the correct equipment is locked out).
Identify hazards and controls before performing a step of a task.	• Put on wire mesh gloves before handling cutter blades. • Use the correct holder to align cutter blades.
Before carrying out a step of a task, identify conditions that can change and the immediate response required while carrying out the step.	• The engine can stall when engaging the clutch on the winch. If the engine stalls, immediately apply the break.

(continued)

Performance Improvement Strategies and Loss Control Measures	Examples
Identify work methods that must **not** be carried out.	• Do **not** place the measuring tools on top of the plastic. The tools will scratch the surface.
Determine the standards of performance for each step of the task so you understand the performance expected and can assess the effectiveness of your actions.	• Use measures of quality, quantity, time, and timeliness (e.g., setpoints, ranges of operation, torque, composition, accuracy of cuts, change in equipment operating status, schedule).
Determine equipment operating limits and what to do if the limits are exceeded.	• If the cylinder temperature reaches 100ºC, open the cooler louvers.
Identify work methods that save effort.	• When balancing equipment, place the temporary counterweight where the permanent counterweight will be mounted to eliminate the need for additional calculations.
Identify strategies that make carrying out a step of a task more efficient.	• When mounting a shaft that has needle bearings, use a sticky substance such as STP to hold the bearings in place.
Identify work methods that are efficient.	• When washing equipment, start at the top and wash downwards.
Identify ways to reduce waste and costs.	• Save the cut-off ends to be used as braces after the wall is erected.
Communicate conditions, actions, and events that are required by other people and to provide a historical record.	• Enter the pump start time in the log book.

LEARNING ACTIVITY 10

Using LO-PEMEO

This learning activity will help you develop your skills to continually apply the LO-PEMEO thinking strategy to any activities that you do.

1. To use the LO-PEMEO strategy for identifying what is important to corporate, job, and your performance, you must examine the five domains to determine if there is any potential for loss or opportunity for optimization.

    a. true
    b. false

2. When you recognize that a condition, action, or event could affect a LO-PEMEO category (e.g., L-P, O-P), you should _____.

    a. investigate further to determine if there is potential for loss or opportunities for optimization
    b. determine the controls to reduce the risk of loss and/ or improve efficiency and effectiveness
    c. do a mental search to determine if other LO-PEMEO categories are affected
    d. all of the above
    e. b and c only

3. Think of a task and record it in the space provided in the following table.

    a. In the first column of the table, write the first five steps to the task.
    b. For each step, suggest standards for performing the step and write your answer in the second column.
    c. For each step, apply LO-PEMEO to identify if conditions, actions, and/or events have the potential for loss or opportunities for optimization. Put your answers in the appropriate column(s).
    d. Suggest control measures for steps that have an entry in either/or the loss and/or optimization column(s).

Task: _____

Steps	Standards of performance	Condition, action, or event causing loss	Opportunity for optimization	Controls
LO-PEMEO Loss/Optimization Analysis				
1				
2				
3				
4				
5				

Section 8

Summary of the Thinking Strategies

All of the thinking strategies addressed in this book place a strong emphasis on asking questions—first of yourself and then of others if you don't have all the answers. By asking yourself questions, you:
- remain vigilant in doing your work
- are able to determine what is important to doing your work
- are able to predict actions, conditions, and events that can potentially create a loss or an opportunity for optimization
- work safely, effectively, and efficiently
- produce exemplary results with the least amount of effort and minimal waste of resources
- contribute effectively to job and corporate performance
- can perform at an exemplary level

Process and Strategies	Descriptions
Applying basic business process	• Discover, Decide, Deliver: gets customer confirmation of each step of the business process.
Using corporate goals	• Identifies what is important to the corporation and the job. Corporate goals help you focus your efforts on issues considered important to your job and department.

(continued)

MetaThink™

Process and Strategies	Descriptions
Assessing issues from different organizational perspectives	• Provides a means of determining how other people view a specific situation and what is important to them.
Using variables	• Helps you understand your work and work environment. Variables can be identified for all domains of PEMEO. Change is an important factor when dealing with variables.
Using reasons, consequences, and causes	• Conditions, actions, and events (effects) define an important part of the work environment. • Reasons provide the motive and explanation of the effects. • In organizations, consequences that are important are those that relate to PEMEO. • Causes provide an explanation for unplanned effects. The root cause must be determined and corrective action taken to achieve a long-term solution to a problem.
Conducting a Loss/ Optimization analysis using LO-PEMEO	• The LO-PEMEO strategy is applied to each step of a procedure to identify potential losses and opportunities for optimization. • Controls are used to minimize loss and ensure the effectiveness and efficiency of work.

Job Aid

Critical Thinking Questions

Business Process
• What are the customer's expectations and concerns for the service or product?
• What are the must have criteria for options?
• What are the other criteria for making a decision as to the best option?
• What is the priority of the other criteria for making a selection of the options?
• Have I confirmed the customer's expectations of the service or product?
• Do all the options meet the must have criteria?
• Are there any negative implications for an option suggested by the customer?
• Have I confirmed the customer's decision in choosing a specific service or product?
• Are there any problems in the delivery of the service or product?
• Have I and others responded effectively to the customer's concerns?

(continued)

Business Process

- Have I confirmed with the customer any changes he or she wants?
- Is the customer satisfied with the service or product?
- Have I confirmed the customer's level of satisfaction?
- What can I do better in the future to deliver the services and products?

Corporate Goals

Generic Corporate Goals

- health and safety
- environment
- regulatory compliance
- corporate policies
- equipment optimization
- equipment life and reliability
- energy consumption
- material optimization
- minimizing losses
- controlling costs
- customer satisfaction
- public image
- public disruption
- teamwork
- communication
- decision making

- What are the corporate goals for my job and department?
- What is the priority of the corporate goals?

Different Job Perspectives

- If I were that person with his/her skills, capabilities, education, experience, beliefs, values, and personal attributes, how would I view the issue?
- Within that person's roles and responsibilities, how important is this issue?
- What are that person's needs, wants, expectations, goals, concerns, and issues?

Variables
<ul><li>What input, process, and output variables are important to my job?</li><li>Is/are the variable(s) static or dynamic?</li><li>Is/are the variable(s) controllable or non-controllable?</li><li>How do I measure the variables?</li><li>What are the agents of cause and the workplace conditions, actions, and events that can lead to or create a hazardous situation?</li><li>What is the desired quality of results?</li><li>How can I do my job more effectively?</li><li>What is the most efficient way to carry out the work?</li><li>What types of decision do I have to make to meet corporate goals?</li><li>What are the variables that affect function and application of a piece of equipment?</li><li>How does the equipment create change?</li><li>What are the minimum, maximum, and optimal settings for the equipment variables?</li><li>What can cause damage to the equipment?</li><li>What affects the reliability of the equipment?</li><li>What affects equipment life?</li><li>What is the most effective way to operate the equipment?</li><li>What is the most efficient way to operate the equipment?</li><li>What changes must be made to materials to achieve the desired quality of results?</li><li>Which material variables must not be changed as a result of work or technical processes?</li><li>What are the material input variables that can affect the efficiency of work or technical processes and quality of results?</li><li>What work and/or process changes made to materials affect the quality of results?</li></ul>

(continued)

Variables

- How can materials get damaged?
- Could the materials have a negative impact on PEMEO?
- How can the use of materials be optimized?
- Could the materials cause harm to the environment?
- What is the proper way to dispose of waste materials?
- What are my roles and responsibilities?
- What are my lines and limits of authority?
- What is important to my job and the organization?
- What corporate goals are important to my job?
- How does my work affect corporate goals?
- How does my work affect others?
- What are the expectations for the work that I do?

Note: *Each book in The Exemplary Worker series has a comprehensive list of questions for the specific category that the book addresses.*

Reasons, Causes, Consequences

- What are the conditions, actions, and events (effect) happening in the workplace?
- What are the immediate reasons relating to PEMEO that have created the conditions, actions, and events?
- What are the corporate reasons for the conditions, actions, and events?
- Why... ?
- What are or could be the consequences for PEMEO?
- What if there is a change to conditions, actions, or events and what would be the consequences?
- If there is a change in conditions, actions, and events, how can I minimize the negative impact on PEMEO?
- What are the immediate causes for changes in the workplace?
- What is the root cause for the changes?
- What can be done to prevent the incident from occurring again?
- What can be done to minimize the consequences if an incident occurs again?

Conducting a Loss/Optimization Analysis Using LO-PEMEO

- What are the criteria for assessing a task for potential loss and optimization opportunities?

  Note: a comprehensive list of criteria can be made by combining the critical questions from each *Exemplary Worker* book. The combined list can be made more specific by expanding the *SafeThink* list to include the agents of cause for Objects, Motion, and Force:
  - 7 agents of cause for stationary objects
  - 10 agents of cause for motion
  - 6 agents of cause for force

- Using the combined list of questions provides a means of carrying out a thorough and rigorous analysis of the task.

- List the steps for performing the task.

- For each step, ask:
  - Are there any agents of cause?
  - Are there any conditions, actions, or events that can cause a loss to PEMEO?
  - What controls can I use to prevent a loss?
  - Are there opportunities to optimize PEMEO?
  - What controls can I use to optimize PEMEO?

Another book by Gordon D. Shand

Interviewing to Gather Relevant Content for Training

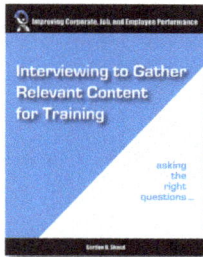

Effective training contributes to business success—
improved corporate, job, and employee performance.
But how do you figure out what training is effective?
This book provides the strategies you need to identify
training that will give you the best return on your
investment in training.

Part A:
- provides criteria and strategies you can use to identify:
  - training content that is relevant
  - what content you should address and not address
- describes pitfalls that you can encounter and ways to resolve these pitfalls

Part B describes an interviewing process where you provide leadership to identify and gather content that is relevant, useful, and practical. You will learn how to:
- help the subject matter expert provide quality content
- select content that is relevant and eliminate content that will not improve performance
- keep the subject matter expert engaged
- structure the content to effectively and efficiently develop training and assessment resources

The suggestions in this book are the accumulated experiences of many training and performance consultants who have encountered the challenges of gathering relevant content and developing effective training.

Who can benefit?

- educational, training, and performance consultants
- training program designers
- instructional designers
- technical writers
- trainers and coaches
- internal staff who develop training

www.ingramcontent.com/pod-product-compliance
Lightning Source LLC
Chambersburg PA
CBHW050240220326
41598CB00047B/7462